FAST & HEALTHY RECIPES

FAST & HEALTHY RECIPES

....

over 100 delicious good-for-you recipes, in no time at all

LORENZ BOOKS

This edition published in 1998 by Lorenz Books
27 West 20th Street, New York, NY 10011

LORENZ BOOKS titles are available for bulk purchase for sales promotion
and for premium use. For details, write or call the sales director,
Anness Publishing Inc., 27 West 20th Street, New York, NY 10011; (800) 354-9657

© Anness Publishing Limited 1995

Lorenz Books is an imprint of Anness Publishing Limited

ISBN 1 85967 666 9

Contributing authors: Catherine Atkinson, Maxine Clarke, Carole Handslip,
Sue Maggs, Annie Nichols, Liz Trigg and Steven Wheeler

Publisher: Joanna Lorenz
Series Editor: Lindsay Porter
Designer: Peter Laws
Photographers: James Duncan, Michelle Garrett and Edward Allwright
Stylists: Madeleine Brehaut, Michelle Garrett and Hilary Guy

The material in this book previously appeared as individual titles in the *Step-by-Step* series

Printed in Hong Kong

1 3 5 7 9 10 8 6 4 2

CONTENTS

INTRODUCTION

In recent years, our diet has come under such scrutiny that we are often confused about what we should or should not eat. It's not surprising that the latest trends in healthy eating are greeted with a certain amount of scepticism. Moderation never seems to be an issue – when advised to reduce fat, this is often translated as cutting out *all* fats, which often leaves us feeling deprived, and more likely to over indulge on the next occasion.

The recipes in this book do not claim to be able to help you lose weight, but neither will they leave you feeling disatisfied, or with cravings for 'forbidden' foods. They are based on the idea that plenty of fresh vegetables and grains, and small amounts of mono-unsaturated fats such as olive oil and that found in oily fish can be combined to provide nutritious meals that are undeniably delicious. Main courses, whether meat based or vegetarian, are hearty and satisfying, and there is a whole range of starters, light meals and accompaniments that can be made quickly, adding an interesting note to any meal. Indulgent desserts and baked treats have not been left out, so you can allow yourself to be tempted, safe in the knowledge that these foods are naturally good for you.

Onions in Toast Cups

Fill crisp bread cups with tender pearl onions tossed in a mustardy glaze.

Serves 4–6

INGREDIENTS
12 thin slices of white bread
8 oz pearl onions or
   shallots
⅔ cup vegetable stock
1 tbsp dry white wine or dry
   sherry
2 turkey bacon rashers, cut into
   thin strips
2 tsp Worcestershire sauce
1 tsp tomato paste
¼ tsp prepared English mustard
salt and freshly ground black pepper
sprigs of Italian parsley, to garnish

pearl onions

stock

white bread

parsley

turkey rashers

1 Preheat the oven to 400°F. Stamp out the bread into rounds with a 3 in fluted cookie cutter and use to line a twelve-cup cupcake pan.

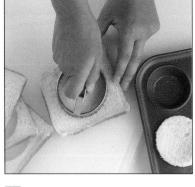

2 Cover each bread case with non-stick baking paper, and fill with baking beans or rice. Bake blind for 5 minutes in the preheated oven. Remove the paper and beans and continue to bake for a further 5 minutes, until lightly browned and crisp.

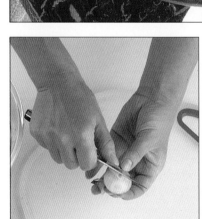

3 Meanwhile, put the pearl onions in a bowl and cover with boiling water. Leave for 3 minutes, then drain and rinse under cold water. Trim off their top and root ends and slip them out of their skins.

4 Simmer the onions and stock in a covered saucepan for 5 minutes. Uncover and cook, stirring occasionally until the stock has reduced entirely. Add all the remaining ingredients, except the parsley. Cook for 2-3 minutes. Fill the toast cups with the deviled onions. Serve hot, garnished with sprigs of Italian parsley.

Mini Pizzas

For a quick supper dish try these delicious little pizzas made with fresh and sun-dried tomatoes.

Makes 4

INGREDIENTS

1 × 5 oz package pizza mix
8 halves sun-dried tomatoes in olive oil, drained
½ cup black olives, pitted
8 oz ripe tomatoes, sliced
¼ cup goat cheese
2 tbsp fresh basil leaves

basil

tomatoes

sun-dried tomatoes

black olives

goat cheese

1 Preheat the oven to 400°F. Make up the pizza base following the instructions on the side of the package.

2 Divide the dough into 4 and roll each piece out to a 5 in disc. Place on a lightly oiled cookie sheet.

3 Place the sun-dried tomatoes and olives in a blender or food processor and blend until smooth. Spread the mixture evenly over the pizza bases.

4 Top with the tomato slices and crumble over the goat cheese. Bake for 10–15 minutes. Sprinkle with the fresh basil and serve.

Crunchy Baked Mushrooms with Dill Dip

These crispy-coated bites are ideal as an informal starter or served with drinks.

Serves 4–6

INGREDIENTS
2 cups fresh fine white bread
    crumbs
1½ tbsp finely grated sharp Cheddar
    cheese
1 tsp paprika
8 oz button mushrooms
2 egg whites

FOR THE TOMATO AND DILL DIP
4 ripe tomatoes
½ cup cottage cheese
4 tbsp natural low fat yogurt
1 garlic clove, crushed
2 tbsp chopped fresh dill
salt and freshly ground black pepper
sprig of fresh dill, to garnish

paprika

mushrooms

dill

tomatoes

bread crumbs

cottage cheese

1 Preheat the oven to 375°F. Mix together the bread crumbs, cheese and paprika in a bowl.

2 Wipe the mushrooms clean and trim the stems, if necessary. Lightly whisk the egg whites with a fork, until frothy.

3 Dip each mushroom into the egg whites, then into the bread crumb mixture. Repeat until all the mushrooms are coated.

4 Put the mushrooms on a non-stick baking sheet. Bake in the preheated oven for 15 minutes, or until tender and the coating has turned golden and crunchy.

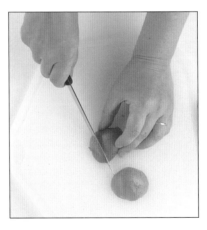

5 Meanwhile, to make the dip, plunge the tomatoes into a saucepan of boiling water for 1 minute, then into a saucepan of cold water. Slip off the skins. Halve, remove the seeds and cores and roughly chop the flesh.

6 Put the cottage cheese, yogurt, garlic clove and dill into a mixing bowl and combine well. Season to taste. Stir in the chopped tomatoes. Spoon the mixture into a serving dish and garnish with a sprig of fresh dill. Serve the mushrooms hot, together with the dip.

Buckwheat Blinis

These delectable light pancakes originated in Russia. For a special occasion, serve with a small glass of chilled vodka.

Serves 4

INGREDIENTS
1 tsp easy-blend dry yeast
1 cup skim or low-fat milk, warmed
⅓ cup buckwheat flour
⅓ cup flour
2 tsp sugar
pinch of salt
1 egg, separated
oil, for frying

FOR THE AVOCADO CREAM
1 large avocado
⅓ cup low fat ricotta cheese
juice of 1 lime

FOR THE PICKLED BEETS
8 oz beets
3 tbsp lime juice
snipped chives, to garnish
cracked black peppercorns, to garnish

beets
avocado
egg
buckwheat flour
lime
chives
ricotta cheese
skim milk

1 Mix the dry yeast with the milk, then mix with the next 4 ingredients and the egg yolk. Cover with a cloth and leave to prove for about 40 minutes. Whisk the egg white until stiff but not dry and fold into the blini mixture.

2 Heat a little oil in a non-stick pan and add a ladleful of batter to make a 4 in pancake. Cook for 2–3 minutes on each side. Repeat with the remaining batter mixture to make 8 blinis.

3 Cut the avocado in half and remove the pit. Peel and place the flesh in a blender with the ricotta cheese and lime juice. Blend until smooth.

4 Peel the beets and shred finely. Mix with the lime juice. To serve, top each blini with a spoonful of avocado cream. Serve with the pickled beets and garnish with snipped chives and cracked black peppercorns.

Soufflé Omelet

This delectable soufflé omelet is light and delicate enough to melt in the mouth.

Serves 1

INGREDIENTS
2 eggs, separated
2 tbsp cold water
1 tbsp chopped fresh coriander
salt and freshly ground black pepper
½ tbsp olive oil
2 tbsp mango chutney
¼ cup Jarlsberg or Swiss cheese, grated

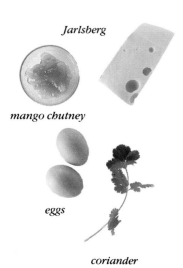

Jarlsberg

mango chutney

eggs

coriander

COOK'S TIP

A light hand is essential to the success of this dish. Do not overmix the egg whites into the yolks or the mixture will be heavy.

1 Beat the egg yolks together with the cold water, coriander and seasoning.

2 Whisk the egg whites until stiff but not dry and gently fold into the egg yolk mixture.

3 Heat the oil in a frying pan, pour in the egg mixture and reduce the heat. Do not stir. Cook until the omelet becomes puffy and golden brown on the underside (carefully lift one edge with a spatula to check).

4 Spoon on the chutney and sprinkle on the Jarlsberg. Fold over and slide onto a warm plate. Eat immediately. (If preferred, before adding the chutney and cheese, place the pan under a hot broiler to set the top.)

Eggplant, Roast Garlic and Red Pepper Pâté

This is a simple pâté of smoky baked eggplant, sweet pink peppercorns and red peppers, with more than a hint of garlic!

Serves 4

INGREDIENTS
3 medium eggplants
2 red peppers
5 whole garlic cloves
1½ tsp pink peppercorns in brine, drained and crushed
2 tbsp chopped fresh coriander

eggplant

garlic

coriander

pink peppercorns

pepper

1 Preheat the oven to 400°F. Arrange the whole eggplants, peppers and garlic cloves on a cookie sheet and place in the oven. After 10 minutes remove the garlic cloves and turn over the eggplants and peppers.

2 Peel the garlic cloves and place in the bowl of a blender.

3 After a further 20 minutes remove the blistered and charred peppers from the oven and place in a paper bag. Leave to cool.

4 After a further 10 minutes remove the eggplants from the oven. Split in half and scoop the flesh into a sieve placed over a bowl. Press the flesh with a spoon to remove the bitter juices.

5 Add the mixture to the garlic in the blender and blend until smooth. Place in a large mixing bowl.

6 Peel and chop the red peppers and stir into the eggplant mixture. Mix in the peppercorns and fresh coriander and serve at once.

Cheese and Onion Pie

This inexpensive supper dish is made substantial with the addition of rolled oats.

Serves 4

INGREDIENTS
2 large onions, thinly sliced
1 garlic clove, crushed
⅔ cup vegetable stock
3 cups rolled oats
1 cup grated Edam cheese
2 tbsp chopped fresh parsley
2 eggs, lightly beaten
1 medium potato, peeled
salt and freshly ground black pepper
coleslaw and tomatoes, halved,
    to serve

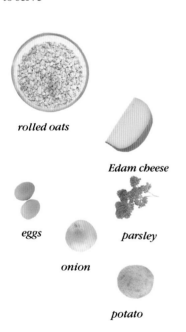

rolled oats

Edam cheese

eggs

parsley

onion

potato

1 Preheat the oven to 350°F. Line the base of a 8 in sandwich pie pan with non-stick baking paper. Put the onions, garlic clove and stock into a heavy-based saucepan and simmer until the stock has reduced entirely.

2 Spread the oats on a baking sheet and toast in the oven for 10 minutes. Mix with the onions, cheese, parsley, eggs, salt and freshly ground black pepper.

3 Thinly slice the potato and use it to line the base of the pan. Spoon in the oat mixture. Cover with a piece of foil.

4 Bake in the preheated oven for 35 minutes. Turn out onto a baking sheet and remove the lining paper. Put under a preheated hot broiler to brown the potatoes. Cut into wedges and serve hot with coleslaw and halved tomatoes.

Potato Gratin

Don't rinse the potato slices before layering because the starch makes a thick sauce during cooking.

Serves 4

INGREDIENTS
1 garlic clove
5 large baking potatoes, unpeeled
3 tbsp freshly grated Parmesan cheese
2½ cups vegetable or low fat chicken stock
pinch of freshly grated nutmeg
salt and freshly ground black pepper

potatoes

Parmesan cheese

stock

1 Preheat the oven to 400°F. Halve the garlic clove and rub over the base and sides of a gratin dish measuring about 8 × 12 in.

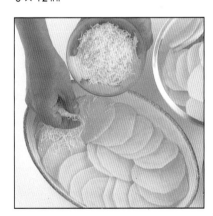

2 Slice the potatoes very thinly and arrange a third of them in the dish. Sprinkle with a little grated cheese, salt and freshly ground black pepper. Pour over some of the stock to prevent the potatoes from discoloring.

3 Continue layering the potatoes and cheese as before, then pour over the rest of the stock. Sprinkle with the nutmeg.

4 Bake in the oven for 1¼-1½ hours or until the potatoes are tender and the tops well browned.

VARIATION

For a potato and onion gratin, thinly slice one medium onion and layer with the potato.

Cucumber and Alfalfa Tortillas

Wheat tortillas are extremely simple to prepare at home. Served with a crisp, fresh salsa, they make a marvelous light lunch or supper dish.

COOK'S TIP

When peeling the avocado be sure to scrape off the bright green flesh from immediately under the skin as this gives the sauce its vivid green color.

Serves 4

INGREDIENTS
2 cups flour, sifted
pinch of salt
3 tbsp olive oil
½–⅔ cup warm water
lime wedges, to garnish

FOR THE SALSA
1 red onion, finely chopped
1 fresh red chili, seeded and finely
  chopped
2 tbsp chopped fresh dill or coriander
½ cucumber, peeled and chopped
6 oz alfalfa sprouts

FOR THE SAUCE
1 large ripe avocado, peeled and
  pitted
juice of 1 lime
2 tbsp soft goat cheese
pinch of paprika

avocado

goat cheese

red chili

cucumber

dill

alfalfa sprouts

1 Mix all the salsa ingredients together in a bowl and set aside.

2 To make the sauce, place the avocado, lime juice and goat cheese in a food processor or blender and blend until smooth. Place in a bowl and cover with plastic wrap. Dust with paprika just before serving.

3 To make the tortillas, place the flour and salt in a food processor, add the oil and blend. Gradually add the water (the amount will vary depending on the type of flour). Stop adding water when a stiff dough has formed. Turn out onto a floured board and knead until smooth. Cover with a damp cloth.

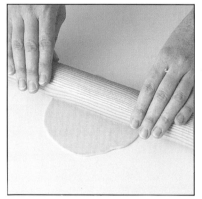

4 Divide the mixture into 8 pieces. Knead each piece for a couple of minutes and form into a ball. Flatten and roll out each ball to a 9 in circle.

5 Heat an ungreased cast-iron pan. Cook 1 tortilla at a time for about 30 seconds on each side. Place the cooked tortillas in a clean dish-towel and repeat until you have 8 tortillas.

6 To serve, spread each tortilla with a spoonful of avocado sauce, top with salsa and roll up. Garnish with lime wedges.

Cheese-stuffed Pears

These pears, with their scrumptious creamy topping, make a sublime dish when served with a simple salad.

Serves 4

INGREDIENTS
¼ cup ricotta cheese
¼ cup Saga blue cheese
1 tbsp honey
½ celery stalk, finely sliced
8 green olives, pitted and roughly
  chopped
4 dates, pitted and cut into thin strips
pinch of paprika
4 ripe pears
⅔ cup apple juice

honey

pear

apple juice

dates

Saga blue

celery

olives

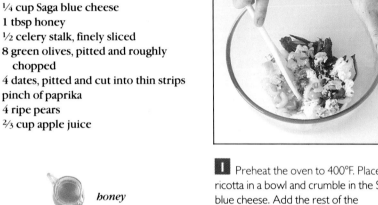

1 Preheat the oven to 400°F. Place the ricotta in a bowl and crumble in the Saga blue cheese. Add the rest of the ingredients except for the pears and apple juice and mix well.

2 Halve the pears lengthwise and use a melon baller to remove the cores. Place in a ovenproof dish and divide the filling equally between them.

3 Pour in the apple juice and cover the dish with foil. Bake for 20 minutes or until the pears are tender.

4 Remove the foil and place the dish under a hot broiler for 3 minutes. Serve immediately.

COOK'S TIP
Choose ripe pears in season such as Bartlett or Comice.

Nutty Chicken Balls

Serve these as a first course with the lemon sauce, or make into smaller balls and serve on wooden sticks as canapés.

Serves 4

INGREDIENTS
12 oz boneless chicken
½ cup unsalted pistachio nuts, finely chopped
1 tbsp lemon juice
2 eggs, beaten
all-purpose flour, for shaping
½ cup blanched chopped almonds
¾ cup dried bread crumbs
salt and freshly ground black pepper

FOR THE LEMON SAUCE
⅔ cup fresh or canned chicken stock
1¼ cups low fat cream cheese
1 tbsp lemon juice
1 tbsp chopped fresh parsley
1 tbsp snipped fresh chives

chopped almonds

minced chicken

chives

pistachio nuts

lemon

bread crumbs

parsley

cream cheese

1 Skin and grind or chop the chicken finely. Mix with salt and freshly ground black pepper, pistachio nuts, lemon juice, and one beaten egg.

2 Shape into sixteen small balls with floured hands (use a spoon as a guide, so that all the balls are roughly the same size). Roll the balls in the remaining beaten egg and coat with the almonds first and then the dried bread crumbs, pressing on firmly. Chill until ready to cook.

3 Preheat the oven to 375°F. Place at regular intervals on a greased baking sheet and bake for about 15 minutes or until golden brown and crisp.

4 To make the lemon sauce, gently heat the chicken stock and cream cheese together in a pan, whisking until smooth. Add the lemon juice, herbs and season to taste. Serve with the chicken balls.

Bruschetta al Pomodoro

Bruschetta is an Italian garlic bread made with the best-quality olive oil you can find and pugliese, a coarse country bread, or ciabatta. Here, chopped tomatoes are added too.

Makes 2

INGREDIENTS
2 large thick slices coarse country
    bread
1 large garlic clove
4 tbsp extra-virgin olive oil
2 ripe tomatoes, skinned and chopped
salt and pepper
1 sprig fresh basil, to garnish

country bread

tomatoes

garlic

1 Toast the bread on both sides.

2 Peel the garlic clove and squash with the flat side of a knife blade.

3 Rub the squashed garlic clove over the toast.

4 Drizzle half the olive oil over the toasted bread.

5 Top with the tomatoes, season well, and drizzle over the remaining oil. Place under the broiler to heat through, then garnish with a sprig of basil and eat immediately.

PLAIN BRUSCHETTA
Rub a crushed garlic clove over untoasted bread, drizzle with oil and then toast.

Focaccia with Hot Artichokes and Olives

Focaccia makes an excellent base for different broiled toppings. Artichoke hearts bottled in oil are the best type to use for this.

Makes 3

INGREDIENTS
4 tbsp olive paste
3 mini focaccia
1 small red bell pepper, halved and seeded
10 oz bottled or canned artichoke hearts, drained
3 oz pepperoni, sliced
1 tsp dried oregano

pepper

mini focaccia

oregano

pepperoni

artichoke hearts

1 Preheat the oven to 425°F. Spread the olive paste over the focaccia. Broil the bell pepper till blackened, put in a plastic bag, seal and allow to cool for 10 minutes. Skin the pepper and cut into strips.

2 Cut the artichoke hearts in quarters and arrange over the paste with the pepperoni.

3 Sprinkle over the bell pepper strips and the oregano. Place in the oven for 5–10 minutes until heated through.

OLIVE FOCACCIA

Focaccia is an Italian flat bread made with olive oil and often with olives as well. The amount of water needed varies with the type of flour used, so you may need a little less – or a little more – than the given quantity.

Makes 2 loaves

4 cups bread flour
1 tsp salt
1 tsp dried yeast
1¼ cups warm water
pinch of sugar
4 tbsp olive oil
1 cup black olives, pitted and roughly chopped
½ tsp dried oregano

Mix the flour and salt together in a mixing bowl. Put the yeast in a small bowl and mix with half the water and a pinch of sugar to help activate the yeast. Leave for about 10 minutes until dissolved. Add the yeast mixture to the flour along with the oil, olives, and remaining water and mix to a soft

dough, adding a little more water if necessary.

Turn the dough out on to a floured surface and knead for 5 minutes until it is smooth and elastic. Place in a mixing bowl, cover with a damp dish towel and leave in a warm place to rise for about 2 hours or until doubled in size.

Preheat the oven to 425°F. Turn the dough out on to a floured surface and knead again for a few minutes. Divide into 2 portions, then roll out each to a thickness of ½ in in either a round or oblong shape. Place on an oiled baking sheet using a floured rolling pin to lift the dough. Make indentations all over the surface using your fingertips and sprinkle with the oregano. Bake in the oven for about 15–20 minutes.

FOCACCIA WITH MOZZARELLA AND SUN-DRIED TOMATOES

Spread the focaccia with 3 tbsp chopped sun-dried tomatoes. Slice 8 oz mozzarella cheese and arrange over the top. Sprinkle with 8 pitted and quartered black olives, and heat through in the oven as for the main recipe.

MINI FOCACCIA

Divide the dough into 6 balls. On a floured surface roll these out to 6 in circles. Finish as for Olive Focaccia, baking for 12–15 minutes.

Ham and Asparagus Slice

Be creative in your arrangement of the ingredients here. You could make ham fingers, or wrap the asparagus in the ham, or use different meats such as salami, mortadella or Black Forest ham.

Makes 4

INGREDIENTS
12 asparagus spears
½ cup low fat cream cheese
4 slices rye bread
4 slices ham
few leaves curly endive
2 tbsp mayonnaise
4 radish roses, to garnish

rye bread

curly endive

ham

asparagus

1 Cook the asparagus until tender, drain, pat dry with paper towels and cool.

2 Spread cream cheese over the rye bread and arrange the ham in folds over the top.

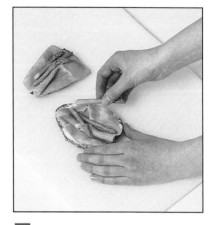

3 Lay 3 asparagus spears on each sandwich.

4 Arrange curly endive on top of the spears and spoon over some mayonnaise.

5 Garnish with radish roses and serve extra mayonnaise separately in a small bowl if liked.

SALAMI AND COTTAGE CHEESE SLICE

Omit the asparagus. Arrange 3 salami slices on top with a spoonful of cottage cheese and chopped fresh chives. Garnish with watercress, chives and chive flowers.

English Muffins with Sole, Spinach and Mushrooms

English muffins, frozen spinach and a few mushrooms form the beginning of this nourishing fish course. Any flatfish will do, although sole works best of all.

Serves 2

INGREDIENTS
½ cup low fat spread
1 medium onion, chopped
4 oz brown button mushrooms, sliced
2 fresh thyme sprigs, chopped
10 oz frozen leaf spinach, thawed
3 lb sole or plaice to yield 1½ lb
   skinned fillet
2 white English muffins, split
4 tbsp low fat crème fraîche
salt and freshly ground black pepper

1 Heat 4 tbsp of the low fat spread in a saucepan and add the onion. Cook over a gentle heat until soft but not coloured.

2 Add the mushrooms and thyme, cover and cook for a further 2–3 minutes. Remove the lid and increase the heat to drive off excess moisture.

English muffins

spinach

crème fraîche

thyme

sole

onion

3 Using the back of a large spoon, press the thawed frozen spinach in a sieve to extract the moisture.

4 Heat a further 2 tbsp low fat spread in a saucepan, add the spinach, heat through and season to taste.

5 Melt the remaining low fat spread in a large frying pan, season the fillets and, with skin side uppermost, cook for 4 minutes, turning once.

COOK'S TIP

Approximately half of the weight of flatfish is bone, so if buying your fish whole, ask the fishmonger to give you the correct weight of boned fish.

6 Toast the muffins. Divide the fillets between them, top with spinach and a layer of mushrooms, then finish with a spoonful of crème fraîche.

Roquefort and Pear

Roquefort is delicious served with pear, but other blue cheeses such as Stilton or Cambozola can be used instead. Toasted brioche makes a good base but must be eaten straight away as it becomes soft once filled.

Makes 4

INGREDIENTS
4 slices brioche loaf
½ cup low fat cottage cheese
few sprigs arugula
4 oz Roquefort cheese, sliced
1 ripe pear, quartered, cored and sliced
juice of ½ lemon
4 pecan nuts, to garnish
viola flowers, to garnish (optional)

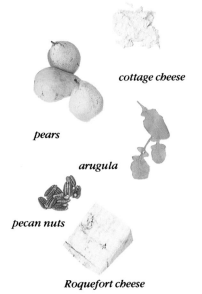

cottage cheese

pears

arugula

pecan nuts

Roquefort cheese

1 Toast the brioche and spread with the cottage cheese.

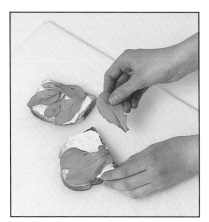

2 Arrange arugula leaves on top of the cheese.

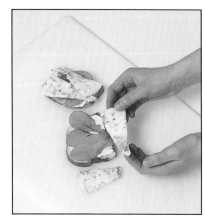

3 Place the sliced Roquefort on top.

4 Brush the pear slices with lemon juice to prevent discoloration.

5 Arrange the pear slices, overlapping, in a fan shape on the cheese.

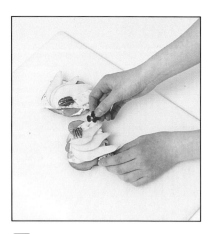

6 Garnish with pecan nuts (whole or chopped) and a viola flower if you wish.

Guacamole with Crudités

This fresh-tasting spicy dip is made using peas instead of the traditional avocados.

Serves 4–6

INGREDIENTS
2¼ cups frozen peas,
    defrosted
1 garlic clove, crushed
2 scallions, trimmed and
    chopped
1 tsp finely grated rind and juice
    of 1 lime
½ tsp ground cumin
dash of Tabasco sauce
1 tbsp reduced calorie
    mayonnaise
2 tbsp chopped fresh cilantro
salt and freshly ground black pepper
pinch of paprika and lime slices,
    to garnish

FOR THE CRUDITÉS
6 baby carrots
2 celery stalks
1 red-skinned apple
1 pear
1 tbsp lemon or lime juice
6 baby corn

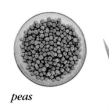

peas

vegetables

1 Put the peas, garlic clove, scallions, lime rind and juice, cumin, Tabasco sauce, mayonnaise and salt and freshly ground black pepper into a food processor or a blender for a few minutes and process until smooth.

2 Add the chopped cilantro and process for a few more seconds. Spoon into a serving bowl, cover with plastic wrap and chill in the refrigerator for 30 minutes, to let the flavors develop.

3 For the crudités, trim and peel the carrots. Halve the celery stalks lengthwise and trim into sticks, the same length as the carrots. Quarter, core and thickly slice the apple and pear, then dip into the lemon or lime juice. Arrange with the baby corn on a platter.

4 Sprinkle the paprika over the guacamole and garnish with lime slices. Serve with the crudités.

Minted Melon and Grapefruit Cocktail

Melon is always a popular starter. Here the flavor is complemented by the refreshing taste of citrus fruit and a simple dressing.

Serves 4

INGREDIENTS
1 small cantaloupe, weighing about
   2¼ lb
2 pink grapefruits
1 yellow grapefruit
1 tsp Dijon mustard
1 tsp raspberry or sherry vinegar
1 tsp honey
1 tbsp chopped fresh mint
sprigs of fresh mint, to garnish

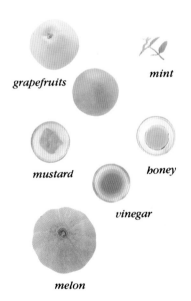

grapefruits   *mint*

mustard   *honey*

vinegar

melon

1 Halve the melon and remove the seeds with a teaspoon. With a melon baller, carefully scoop the flesh into balls.

2 With a sharp knife, peel the grapefruit and remove all the white pith. Remove the segments by cutting between the membranes, holding the fruit over a small bowl to catch any juices.

3 Whisk the mustard, vinegar, honey, chopped mint and grapefruit juices together in a mixing bowl. Add the melon balls together with the grapefruit and mix well. Chill for 30 minutes.

4 Ladle into four dishes and serve garnished with a sprig of fresh mint.

Minestrone

A classic substantial winter soup originally from Milan, but found in various versions around the Mediterranean coasts of Italy and France. Cut the vegetables as roughly or as small as you like. Add freshly grated Parmesan cheese just before serving.

Serves 6–8

INGREDIENTS
2 cups dried white beans
2 tbsp olive oil
2 oz bacon, diced
2 large onions, sliced
2 garlic cloves, crushed
2 medium carrots, diced
3 celery sticks, sliced
14 oz canned chopped tomatoes
10 cups beef stock
12 oz potatoes, diced
1½ cups small pasta shapes
   (macaroni, stars, shells, etc)
½ lb green cabbage, thinly sliced
6 oz fine green beans, sliced
¾ cup frozen peas
3 tbsp chopped fresh parsley
salt and pepper
freshly grated Parmesan cheese,
   to serve

1 Cover the beans with cold water and leave to soak overnight.

2 Heat the oil in a large saucepan and add the bacon, onions, and garlic. Cover and cook gently for 5 minutes, stirring occasionally, until soft.

3 Add the carrots and celery and cook for 2–3 minutes until softening.

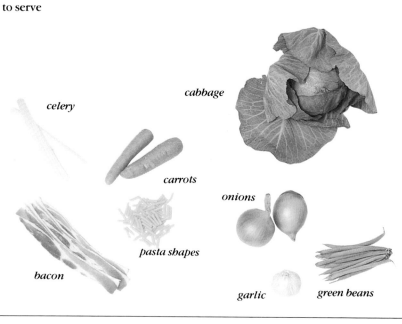

celery

cabbage

carrots

onions

pasta shapes

bacon

garlic

green beans

4 Drain the beans and add to the pan with the tomatoes and stock. Cover and simmer for 2–2½ hours, until the beans are tender.

5 Add the potatoes 30 minutes before the soup is finished.

VARIATION

To make Soupe au Pistou from the South of France, stir in a basil, garlic and pine nut sauce (pesto or pistou) just before serving.

6 Add the pasta, cabbage, beans, peas, and parsley 15 minutes before the soup is ready. Season to taste and serve with a bowl of freshly grated Parmesan cheese.

Red Onion and Beet Soup

This beautiful vivid ruby-red soup will look stunning at any dinner party.

Serves 4–6

INGREDIENTS
1 tbsp olive oil
12 oz red onions, sliced
2 garlic cloves, crushed
10 oz cooked beets, cut into
    thin sticks
5 cups fresh vegetable stock or water
1 cup cooked soup pasta
2 tbsp raspberry vinegar
salt and freshly ground black pepper
low fat yogurt or ricotta cheese, to
    garnish
snipped chives, to garnish

garlic

red onion

beets

pasta

chives

1 Heat the olive oil and add the onions and garlic.

2 Cook gently for about 20 minutes or until soft and tender.

3 Add the beets, stock or water, cooked pasta shapes and vinegar and heat through. Season to taste.

4 Ladle into bowls. Top each one with a spoonful of yogurt or ricotta cheese and sprinkle with chives.

COOK'S TIP

Try substituting cooked barley for the pasta to give extra nuttiness.

Cauliflower, Flageolet and Fennel Seed Soup

The sweet, anise-liquorice flavor of the fennel seeds gives a delicious edge to this hearty soup.

Serves 4–6

INGREDIENTS
1 tbsp olive oil
1 garlic clove, crushed
1 onion, chopped
2 tsp fennel seeds
1 cauliflower, cut into small florets
2 × 14 oz cans flageolet beans,
   drained and rinsed
5 cups fresh vegetable stock or water
salt and freshly ground black pepper
chopped fresh parsley, to garnish
toasted slices of French bread, to
   serve

flageolet beans

French bread

onion

garlic

cauliflower

fennel seeds

parsley

1 Heat the olive oil. Add the garlic, onion and fennel seeds and cook gently for 5 minutes or until softened.

2 Add the cauliflower, half of the beans and the stock or water.

3 Bring to a boil. Reduce the heat and simmer for 10 minutes or until the cauliflower is tender.

4 Pour the soup into a blender and blend until smooth. Stir in the remaining beans and season to taste. Reheat and pour into bowls. Sprinkle with chopped parsley and serve with toasted slices of French bread.

Italian Bean and Pasta Soup

A thick and hearty soup which, followed by bread and cheese, makes a substantial lunch.

Serves 6

INGREDIENTS

1½ cups dried white beans, soaked
    overnight in cold water
7½ cups chicken stock or water
1 cup medium pasta shells
4 tbsp olive oil, plus extra to serve
2 garlic cloves, crushed
4 tbsp chopped fresh parsley
salt and pepper

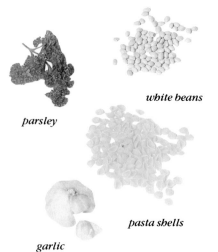

parsley

white beans

pasta shells

garlic

1 Drain the beans and place in a large saucepan with the stock or water. Simmer, half-covered, for 2–2½ hours or until tender.

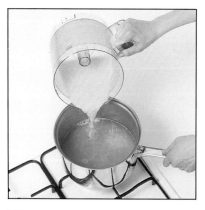

2 Liquidize half the beans and a little of their cooking liquid, then stir into the remaining beans in the pan.

3 Add the pasta and simmer gently for 15 minutes until tender. (Add extra water or stock if the soup seems too thick.)

4 Heat the oil in a small pan and fry the garlic until golden. Stir into the soup with the parsley and season well with salt and pepper. Ladle into individual bowls and drizzle each with a little extra olive oil.

Italian Vegetable Soup

The success of this clear soup depends on the quality of the stock, so use homemade vegetable stock rather than bouillon cubes.

Serves 4

INGREDIENTS
1 small carrot
1 baby leek
1 celery stalk
2 oz green cabbage
3¾ cups vegetable
   stock
1 bay leaf
1 cup cooked cannellini beans, rinsed
   and drained
⅕ cup soup pasta, such as tiny shells,
   bows, stars or elbows
salt and freshly ground black pepper
snipped fresh chives, to garnish

stock

cabbage

bay leaf

chives

baby leek

celery

carrot

pasta

1 Cut the carrot, leek and celery into 2 in long julienne strips. Slice the cabbage very finely.

2 Put the stock and bay leaf into a large saucepan and bring to a boil. Add the carrot, leek and celery, cover and simmer for 6 minutes.

3 Add the cabbage, beans and pasta shapes. Stir, then simmer uncovered for a further 4-5 minutes, or until the vegetables and pasta are tender.

4 Remove the bay leaf and season to taste. Ladle into four soup bowls and garnish with snipped chives. Serve immediately.

Tabbouleh with Fennel and Pomegranate

A fresh salad originating in the Middle East, with the added crunchiness of fennel and sweet pomegranate seeds. It is perfect for a summer lunch.

Serves 6

INGREDIENTS
1 cup bulgur wheat
2 fennel bulbs
1 small fresh red chili, seeded and
   finely chopped
1 celery stalk, finely sliced
30 ml/2 tbsp olive oil
finely grated rind and juice of 2
   lemons
6–8 scallions, chopped
6 tbsp chopped fresh mint
6 tbsp chopped fresh parsley
1 pomegranate, seeds removed
salt and freshly ground black pepper

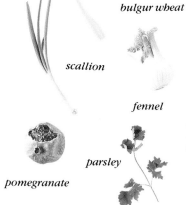
pomegranate

lemon

red chili

celery

bulgur wheat

scallion

fennel

parsley

mint

1 Place the bulgur wheat in a bowl and pour over enough cold water to cover. Leave to stand for 30 minutes.

2 Drain the wheat through a sieve, pressing out any excess water using a spoon.

3 Halve the fennel bulbs and cut into very fine slices.

4 Mix all the remaining ingredients together, including the soaked bulgur wheat and fennel. Season well, cover, and set aside for 30 minutes before serving.

Buckwheat Couscous with Goat Cheese and Celery

Couscous is made from cracked, partially cooked wheat, which is dried and then reconstituted in water or stock. It tastes of very little by itself, but carries the flavor of other ingredients very well.

Serves 4

INGREDIENTS
1 egg
2 tbsp olive oil
1 small bunch scallions, chopped
2 celery stalks, sliced
1 cup couscous
½ cup buckwheat
3 tbsp chopped fresh parsley
finely grated zest of ½ lemon
¼ cup chopped walnuts, toasted
5 oz strongly flavored goat
  cheese
salt and freshly ground black pepper
Romaine lettuce leaves, to serve

buckwheat

celery

egg

goat
cheese

parsley

walnuts

1 Boil the egg for 10 minutes, cool, peel and set aside. Heat the oil in a saucepan and add the scallions and celery. Cook for 2–3 minutes until soft.

2 Add the couscous and buckwheat and cover with 2½ cups of boiling salted water. Cover and return to a simmer. Remove from the heat and allow the couscous to soften and absorb the water for about 3 minutes. Transfer the mixture to a large bowl.

3 Grate the hard-boiled egg finely into a small bowl and add the chopped parsley, lemon zest and walnuts. Fold into the couscous, season, and crumble in the goat cheese. Mix well and then turn out into a shallow dish. Serve warm with a salad of Romaine lettuce.

VARIATION
Couscous is ideal as a filling for pita breads when accompanied with crisp salad leaves.

Red Bell Pepper Polenta with Sunflower Salsa

This recipe is inspired by Italian and Mexican cookery. Cornmeal polenta is a staple food in Italy, served with brightly colored vegetables. Mexican *Pipian* is a salsa made from sunflower seeds, chili and lime.

Serves 4

INGREDIENTS
3 young zucchinis
oil, for greasing
5 cups light vegetable stock
2 cups fine polenta or cornmeal
1 × 7 oz jar red peppers, drained and sliced
4 oz green salad, to serve

FOR THE SUNFLOWER SALSA
3 oz sunflower seeds, toasted
1 cup crustless white bread
scant 1 cup vegetable stock
1 garlic clove, crushed
½ red chili, seeded and chopped
2 tbsp chopped fresh cilantro
1 tsp sugar
1 tbsp lime juice
pinch of salt

1 Bring a saucepan of salted water to a boil. Add the zucchinis and simmer over a low heat for 2–3 minutes. Refresh under cold running water and drain. When they are cool, cut into strips.

2 Lightly oil a 9 in loaf pan and line with a single sheet of waxed paper.

polenta

sunflower seeds

zucchini

limes

red chilies

peppers

cilantro

white bread

3 Bring the vegetable stock to a simmer in a heavy saucepan. Add the polenta in a steady stream, stirring continuously for about 2–3 minutes until thickened.

4 Partly fill the lined pan with the polenta mixture. Layer the sliced zucchinis and peppers over the polenta. Fill the pan with the remaining polenta and leave to set for about 10–15 minutes. Polenta should be served warm or at room temperature.

COOK'S TIP

Sunflower salsa will keep for up to 10 days in the refrigerator. It is delicious poured over a simple dish of pasta.

5 To make the salsa, reduce the sunflower seeds to a thick paste in a food processor. Add the remaining ingredients and combine thoroughly.

6 Turn the warm polenta out onto a board, remove the paper and cut into thick slices with a large wet knife. Serve with the salsa and a green salad.

Chili Bean Bake

The contrasting textures of spicy beans, vegetables and crunchy cornbread topping make this a memorable meal.

Serves 4

INGREDIENTS

1⅓ cups red kidney beans
1 bay leaf
1 large onion, finely chopped
1 garlic clove, crushed
2 celery stalks, sliced
1 tsp ground cumin
1 tsp chili powder
14 oz can chopped tomatoes
1 tbsp tomato paste
1 tsp dried mixed herbs
1 tbsp lemon juice
1 yellow bell pepper, seeded and
   diced
salt and freshly ground black pepper
mixed salad, to serve

FOR THE CORNBREAD TOPPING

1½ cups corn meal
1 tbsp whole wheat flour
1 tsp baking powder
1 egg, beaten
¾ cup skim milk

kidney beans

celery

tomato paste

pepper

1 Soak the beans overnight in cold water. Drain and rinse well. Pour 4 cups of water into a large, heavy-based saucepan together with the beans and bay leaf and boil rapidly for 10 minutes. Lower the heat, cover and simmer for 35–40 minutes, or until the beans are tender.

2 Add the onion, garlic clove, celery, cumin, chili powder, chopped tomatoes, tomato paste and dried mixed herbs. Half-cover the pan with a lid and simmer for a further 10 minutes.

3 Stir in the lemon juice, yellow pepper and seasoning. Simmer for a further 8-10 minutes, stirring occasionally, until the vegetables are just tender. Discard the bay leaf and spoon the mixture into a large casserole.

4 Preheat the oven to 425°F. For the topping, put the corn meal, flour, baking powder and a pinch of salt into a bowl and mix together. Make a well in the center and add the egg and milk. Mix and pour over the bean mixture. Bake in the preheated oven for 20 minutes, or until brown.

Cannellini Bean Purée with Grilled Radicchio

The slightly bitter flavors of the radicchio and chicory make a wonderful marriage with the creamy citrus flavored bean purée.

Serves 4

INGREDIENTS
14 oz can cannellini beans
3 tbsp low fat ricotta cheese
finely grated rind and juice of 1
    large orange
1 tbsp finely chopped fresh rosemary
4 heads of chicory
2 medium radicchio
1 tbsp walnut oil

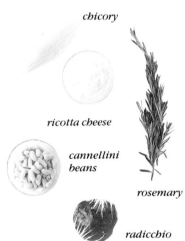

chicory

ricotta cheese

cannellini
beans

rosemary

radicchio

orange

1 Drain the beans, rinse, and drain again. Purée the beans in a blender or food processor with the ricotta cheese, orange juice and rosemary. Set aside.

2 Cut the chicory in half lengthwise.

3 Cut each radicchio into 8 wedges.

4 Lay out the chicory and radicchio on a baking tray and brush with walnut oil. Grill for 2–3 minutes. Serve with the sauce and scatter over the orange rind.

COOK'S TIP
Other suitable beans to use are navy, mung or broad beans.

Pumpkin and Pistachio Risotto

This elegant combination of creamy golden rice and orange pumpkin can be as pale or bright as you like by adding different quantities of saffron.

Serves 4

INGREDIENTS
5 cups fresh vegetable stock or water
generous pinch of saffron threads
2 tbsp olive oil
1 medium onion, chopped
2 garlic cloves, crushed
1 lb arborio rice
2 lb pumpkin, peeled, seeded and cut
 into ¾ in cubes
¾ cup dry white wine
½ oz Parmesan cheese, finely grated
½ cup pistachios
3 tbsp chopped fresh marjoram or
 oregano, plus extra leaves, to
 garnish
salt, freshly grated nutmeg and ground
 black pepper

2 Heat the oil in a large saucepan. Add the onion and garlic and cook gently for about 5 minutes until softened. Add the rice and pumpkin and cook for a few more minutes until the rice looks transparent.

3 Pour in the wine and allow it to boil hard. When it is absorbed add ¼ of the stock and the infused saffron and liquid. Stir constantly until all the liquid is absorbed.

1 Bring the stock or water to a boil and reduce to a low simmer. Ladle a little stock into a small bowl. Add the saffron threads and leave to infuse.

4 Gradually add the stock or water, a ladleful at a time, allowing the rice to absorb the liquid before adding more and stirring all the time. After 20–30 minutes the rice should be golden yellow and creamy, and *al dente* when tested.

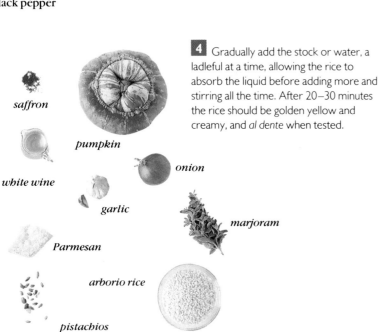

saffron

pumpkin

white wine

garlic

onion

marjoram

Parmesan

arborio rice

pistachios

5 Stir in the Parmesan cheese, cover the pan and leave to stand for 5 minutes.

6 To finish, stir in the pistachios and marjoram or oregano. Season to taste with a little salt, nutmeg and pepper, and scatter over a few extra marjoram or oregano leaves.

COOK'S TIP
Italian arborio rice must be used to make an authentic risotto. Choose unpolished white arborio as it contains more starch.

Lemon and Ginger Spicy Beans

An extremely quick delicious meal, made with canned beans for speed. You probably won't need extra salt as canned beans tend to be already salted.

Serves 4

INGREDIENTS
2 tbsp roughly chopped fresh ginger root
3 garlic cloves, roughly chopped
1 cup cold water
1 tbsp sunflower oil
1 large onion, thinly sliced
1 fresh red chili, seeded and finely chopped
¼ tsp cayenne pepper
2 tsp ground cumin
1 tsp ground coriander
½ tsp ground turmeric
2 tbsp lemon juice
⅓ cup chopped fresh coriander
1 × 14 oz can black-eyed beans, drained and rinsed
1 × 14 oz can adzuki beans, drained and rinsed
1 × 14 oz can navy beans, drained and rinsed
freshly ground black pepper

garlic

red chili

ginger

ground coriander

ground turmeric

ground cumin

navy beans

adzuki beans

black-eyed beans

onion

1 Place the ginger, garlic and 4 tbsp of the cold water in a blender and mix until smooth.

2 Heat the oil in a pan. Add the onion and chili and cook gently for 5 minutes until softened.

3 Add the cayenne pepper, cumin, ground coriander and turmeric and stir-fry for 1 minute.

4 Stir in the ginger and garlic paste from the blender and cook for another minute.

5 Add the remaining water, lemon juice and fresh coriander, stir well and bring to a boil. Cover the pan tightly and cook for 5 minutes.

6 Add all the beans and cook for a further 5–10 minutes. Season with pepper to taste and serve.

Vegetarian Cassoulet

Every town in southwest France has its own version of this popular classic. Warm French bread is all that is needed to complete this hearty vegetable version.

Serves 4–6

INGREDIENTS
2 cups dried navy beans
1 bay leaf
2 onions
3 whole cloves
2 garlic cloves, crushed
1 tsp olive oil
2 leeks, thickly sliced
12 baby carrots
4 oz button mushrooms
14 oz can chopped tomatoes
1 tbsp tomato paste
1 tsp paprika
1 tbsp chopped fresh thyme
2 tbsp chopped fresh parsley
2 cups fresh white bread crumbs
salt and freshly ground black pepper
sprig of fresh thyme, to garnish

COOK'S TIP
If you're short of time use canned navy beans – you'll need two 14 oz cans. Drain, reserving the bean juices and make up to 1⅔ cups with vegetable stock.

1 Soak the beans overnight in plenty of cold water. Drain and rinse under cold running water. Put them in a saucepan together with 7½ cups of cold water and the bay leaf. Bring to a boil and cook rapidly for 10 minutes.

2 Peel one of the onions and spike with cloves. Add to the beans and reduce the heat. Cover and simmer gently for 1 hour, until the beans are almost tender. Drain, reserving the stock but discarding the bay leaf and onion.

3 Chop the remaining onion and put it into a large flameproof casserole together with the garlic cloves and olive oil. Cook gently for 5 minutes, or until softened.

chopped tomatoes

bay leaf

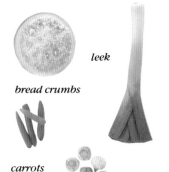
bread crumbs

leek

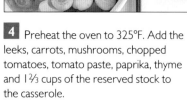

4 Preheat the oven to 325°F. Add the leeks, carrots, mushrooms, chopped tomatoes, tomato paste, paprika, thyme and 1⅔ cups of the reserved stock to the casserole.

carrots   *mushrooms*

5 Bring to a boil, cover and simmer gently for 10 minutes. Stir in the cooked beans and parsley. Season to taste.

6 Sprinkle with the bread crumbs and bake uncovered in the preheated oven for 35 minutes, or until the topping is golden brown and crisp. Serve garnished with a sprig of fresh thyme.

Risotto-stuffed Eggplants with Spicy Tomato Sauce

Eggplants are a challenge to the creative cook and allow for some unusual recipe ideas. Here, they are stuffed and baked with a cheese and pine nut topping.

Serves 4

INGREDIENTS
4 small eggplants
7 tbsp olive oil
1 small onion, chopped
scant 1 cup arborio rice
3⅔ cups ready-made or fresh
   vegetable stock
1 tbsp white wine vinegar
8 fresh basil sprigs, to garnish

FOR THE TOPPING
¼ cup freshly grated Parmesan
   cheese
1 tbsp pine nuts

FOR THE TOMATO SAUCE
1¼ cups crushed tomatoes or
tomato purée
1 tsp mild curry paste
pinch of salt

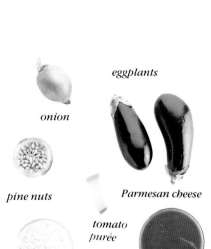

onion
eggplants
pine nuts
Parmesan cheese
tomato purée
rice

COOK'S TIP
Don't be put off by the amount of oil eggplants absorb when cooking. Use olive oil and remember that good oils are low in saturated fat and are believed to fight against heart disease.

1 Preheat the oven to 400°F. Cut the eggplants in half lengthwise and take out their flesh with a small knife. Brush with 2 tbsp of the oil, place on a baking sheet and cook in the preheated oven for 6–8 minutes.

2 Chop the reserved eggplant flesh and heat the remainder of the olive oil in a medium saucepan. Add the eggplant flesh and the onion and cook over a gentle heat for 3–4 minutes until soft.

3 Add the rice, stir in the stock and simmer uncovered for a further 15 minutes. Stir in the vinegar.

4 Increase the oven temperature to 450°F. Spoon the rice into the eggplant skins, top with cheese and pine nuts, and return to the oven to brown for 5 minutes.

5 To make the sauce, combine the crushed tomatoes or tomato purée with the curry paste, heat and add salt to taste.

6 Spoon the sauce onto four large serving plates and position two eggplant halves on each. Garnish with basil sprigs.

Salmon Risotto with Cucumber and Tarragon

Any rice can be used for risotto. The creamiest ones are made with short-grain Arborio and Carnaroli rice but they do take more time. Fresh tarragon and cucumber bring out the flavor of the salmon.

Serves 4

INGREDIENTS

2 tbsp butter
1 small bunch scallions, white part
  only, chopped
½ cucumber, peeled, deseeded
  and chopped
2 cups rice
3¾ cups fresh or canned chicken or
  fish stock
⅔ cup dry white wine
1 lb salmon fillet, skinned
  and diced
3 tbsp chopped fresh tarragon

salmon fillet

butter

cucumber

rice

tarragon

scallions

1 Heat the butter in a large saucepan, and add the scallions and cucumber. Cook for 2–3 minutes without coloring.

2 Add the rice, stock and wine, return to a boil and simmer uncovered for 10 minutes, stirring occasionally.

3 Stir in the diced salmon and tarragon. Continue cooking for a further 5 minutes, then switch off the heat. Cover and leave to stand for 5 minutes before serving.

VARIATION

Long-grain rice can also be used. Choose grains that have not been pre-cooked and reduce the stock to 3⅔ cups, per 2 cups of rice.

Green Lentil and Cabbage Salad

This warm crunchy salad makes a satisfying meal if served with crusty French bread or wholemeal rolls.

Serves 4–6

INGREDIENTS
1 cup green lentils
6 cups cold water
1 garlic clove
1 bay leaf
1 small onion, peeled and studded
   with 2 cloves
1 tbsp olive oil
1 red onion, finely sliced
2 garlic cloves, crushed
1 tbsp thyme leaves
12 oz cabbage, finely shredded
finely grated rind and juice of 1 lemon
1 tbsp raspberry vinegar
salt and freshly ground black pepper

thyme

cabbage

onion

red onion

bay leaf

lemon

garlic

cloves

peppercorns

1 Rinse the lentils in cold water and place in a large pan with the water, peeled garlic clove, bay leaf and clove-studded onion. Bring to a boil and cook for 10 minutes. Reduce the heat, cover the pan and simmer gently for 15–20 minutes. Drain and remove the onion, garlic and bay leaf.

2 Heat the oil in a large pan. Add the red onion, garlic and thyme and cook for 5 minutes until softened.

3 Add the cabbage and cook for 3–5 minutes until just cooked but still crunchy.

4 Stir in the cooked lentils, lemon rind and juice and the raspberry vinegar. Season to taste and serve.

Fruit and Fiber Salad

Fresh, fast and filling, this salad makes a great starter, supper or snack.

Serves 4–6

INGREDIENTS
8 oz red or white cabbage or a
   mixture of both
3 medium carrots
1 pear
1 red-skinned apple
7 oz can lima beans,
   drained
¼ cup chopped dates

FOR THE DRESSING
½ tsp dry English mustard
2 tsp honey
2 tbsp orange juice
1 tsp white wine vinegar
½ tsp paprika
salt and freshly ground black pepper

dates

orange

carrot

lima
beans

cabbage   pear

apple

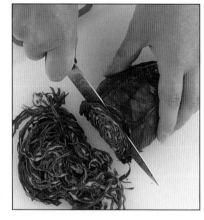

1 Shred the cabbage very finely, discarding any tough stalks.

2 Cut the carrots into very thin strips, about 2 in long.

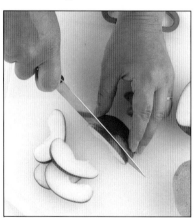

3 Quarter, core and slice the pear and apple, leaving the skin on.

4 Put the fruit and vegetables in a bowl with the beans and dates. Mix well.

5 For the dressing, blend the mustard with the honey until smooth. Add the orange juice, vinegar, paprika and seasoning and mix well.

6 Pour the dressing over the salad and toss to coat. Chill in the refrigerator for 30 minutes before serving.

Stir-fried Chickpeas

Buy canned chickpeas and you will save all the time needed for soaking and then thoroughly cooking dried chickpeas. Served with a crisp green salad, this dish make a filling vegetarian main course for two, or could be served in smaller quantities as a starter or side dish.

Serves 2–4 as an accompaniment

INGREDIENTS
2 tbsp sunflower seeds
1 × 14 oz can chickpeas, drained
    and rinsed
1 tsp chili powder
1 tsp paprika
2 tbsp vegetable oil
1 clove garlic, crushed
7 oz canned chopped tomatoes
8 oz fresh spinach, well washed and
    coarse stalks removed
salt and freshly ground black pepper
2 tsp chili oil

spinach
garlic

sunflower seeds

chickpeas

1 Heat the wok, and then add the sunflower seeds. Dry-fry until the seeds are golden and toasted.

2 Remove the sunflower seeds and set aside. Toss the chickpeas in chili powder and paprika. Remove and reserve.

3 Heat the wok, then add the oil. When the oil is hot, stir-fry the garlic for 30 seconds, add the chickpeas and stir-fry for 1 minute.

4 Stir in the tomatoes and stir-fry for 4 minutes. Toss in the spinach, season well and stir-fry for 1 minute. Drizzle chili oil and scatter sunflower seeds over the vegetables, then serve.

White Bean and Celery Salad

This simple bean salad is a delicious alternative to the potato salad that seems to appear on every picnic spread. If you do not have time to soak and cook dried beans, use canned ones.

Serves 4

INGREDIENTS
1 lb dried white beans (haricot, canellini, navy, or butter beans) or 3 × 14 oz cans white beans
4½ cups vegetable stock, made from a cube
3 stalks celery, cut into ½ in strips
½ cup French dressing
3 tbsp chopped fresh parsley
salt and freshly ground black pepper

parsley

white beans

celery

1 If using dried beans, cover with plenty of cold water and soak for at least 4 hours. Discard the soaking water, then place the beans in a heavy saucepan. Cover with fresh water, bring to a boil, and simmer without a lid for 1½ hours, or until the skins are broken. Cooked beans will squash readily between a thumb and forefinger. Drain the beans. If using canned beans, drain, rinse and use from this stage in the recipe.

COOK'S TIP
Dried beans that have been kept for longer than 6 months will need soaking overnight to lessen their cooking time. As a rule, the less time beans have been kept, the shorter the soaking and cooking time they need. The times given here are suited to freshly purchased beans.

2 Place the cooked beans in a large saucepan. Add the vegetable stock and celery, bring to a boil, cover, and simmer for 15 minutes. Drain thoroughly. Toss the beans with the dressing and leave to cool.

3 Add the chopped parsley and season to taste with salt and pepper.

Thai Fragrant Rice

A lovely, soft, fluffy rice dish, perfumed with fresh lemon grass.

Serves 4

INGREDIENTS
1 piece of lemon grass
2 limes
1 cup brown basmati rice
1 tbsp olive oil
1 onion, chopped
1 in piece of fresh ginger root, peeled and finely chopped
1½ tsp coriander seeds
1½ tsp cumin seeds
3 cups fresh vegetable stock or water
4 tbsp chopped fresh coriander
lime wedges, to serve

onion

lime

ginger

lemon grass

coriander seeds

basmati rice

cumin seeds

coriander

1 Finely chop the lemon grass.

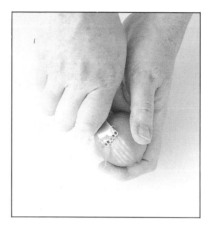

2 Remove the zest from the limes using a zester or fine grater.

3 Rinse the rice in plenty of cold water until the water runs clear. Drain through a sieve.

4 Heat the oil in a large pan and add the onion and spices, lemon grass and lime zest and cook gently for 2–3 minutes.

5 Add the rice and cook for another minute, then add the stock and bring to a boil. Reduce the heat to very low and cover the pan. Cook gently for 30 minutes then check the rice. If it is still crunchy, cover the pan again and leave for a further 3–5 minutes. Remove from the heat.

6 Stir in the fresh coriander, fluff up the grains, cover and leave for 10 minutes. Serve with lime wedges.

COOK'S TIP

Other varieties of rice, such as white basmati or long grain, can be used for this dish but you will need to adjust the cooking times accordingly.

Chinese Jewelled Rice

This rice dish, with its many different, interesting ingredients, can make a meal in itself.

Serves 4

INGREDIENTS
12 oz long grain rice
3 tbsp vegetable oil
1 onion, roughly chopped
4 oz cooked ham, diced
6 oz canned white crabmeat
3 oz canned water chestnuts, drained
   and cut into cubes
4 dried black Chinese mushrooms,
   soaked, drained and cut into dice
4 oz peas, thawed if frozen
2 tbsp oyster sauce
1 tsp sugar

rice

Chinese mushrooms

diced ham

water chestnuts

peas

crabmeat

1 Rinse the rice, then cook for about 10–12 minutes in 2½–3 cups water in a saucepan with a tight-fitting lid. When cooked, refresh under cold water. Heat the wok, then add half the oil. When the oil is hot, stir-fry the rice for 3 minutes, then remove and set aside.

2 Add the remaining oil to the wok. When the oil is hot, cook the onion until softened but not colored.

3 Add the remaining ingredients and stir-fry for 2 minutes.

4 Return the rice to the wok and stir-fry for 3 minutes, then serve.

Nutty Rice and Mushroom Stir-fry

This delicious and substantial supper dish can be eaten hot or cold with salads.

Serves 4–6

INGREDIENTS

12 oz long grain rice
3 tbsp sunflower oil
1 small onion, roughly chopped
8 oz field mushrooms, sliced
½ cup hazelnuts, roughly
   chopped
½ cup pecans, roughly
   chopped
½ cup almonds, roughly
   chopped
4 tbsp fresh parsley, chopped
salt and freshly ground black pepper

rice

almonds

field mushroom

hazelnuts

pecans

1 Rinse the rice, then cook for about 10–12 minutes in 2½–3 cups water in a saucepan with a tight-fitting lid. When cooked, refresh under cold water. Heat the wok, then add half the oil. When the oil is hot, stir-fry the rice for 2–3 minutes. Remove and set aside.

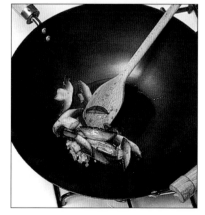

2 Add the remaining oil and stir-fry the onion for 2 minutes until softened.

3 Mix the field mushrooms and stir-fry for 2 minutes.

4 Add all the nuts and stir-fry for 1 minute. Return the rice to the wok and stir-fry for 3 minutes. Season with salt and pepper. Stir in the parsley and serve.

Jamaican Spiced Cod Steaks with Pumpkin Ragout

Spicy hot from Kingston town, this fast fish dish is guaranteed to appeal. The term 'ragout' is taken from the old French verb ragoûter, which means to stimulate the appetite.

COOK'S TIP

This recipe can be adapted using any types of firm pink or white fish that is available, such as haddock, whiting, monkfish, halibut or tuna.

Serves 4

INGREDIENTS
finely grated zest of ½ orange
2 tbsp black peppercorns
1 tbsp allspice berries or Jamaican
  pepper
½ tsp salt
4 × 6 oz cod steaks
groundnut oil, for frying
new potatoes, to serve (optional)
3 tbsp chopped fresh parsley,
  to garnish

FOR THE RAGOUT
2 tbsp groundnut oil
1 medium onion, chopped
1 in fresh ginger root, peeled and
  grated
1 lb fresh pumpkin, peeled, deseeded
  and chopped
3–4 shakes of Tabasco sauce
2 tbsp soft brown sugar
1 tbsp vinegar

pumpkin

cod steaks

ginger

1 To make the ragout, heat the oil in a heavy saucepan and add the onion and ginger. Cover and cook, stirring, for 3–4 minutes until soft.

2 Add the chopped pumpkin, Tabasco sauce, brown sugar and vinegar, cover and cook over a low heat for 10–12 minutes until softened.

3 Combine the orange zest, peppercorns, allspice or Jamaican pepper and salt, then crush coarsely using a pestle and mortar. (Alternatively, coarsely grind the peppercorns in a pepper mill and combine with the zest and seasoning.)

4 Scatter the spice mixture over both sides of the fish and moisten with a sprinkling of oil.

5 Heat a large frying pan and fry the cod steaks for 12 minutes, turning once.

6 Serve the cod steaks with a spoonful of pumpkin ragout and new potatoes, if desired, and garnish the ragout with chopped fresh parsley.

Pickled Herrings with Beet and Apple Relish

Soused or pickled herrings are delicious with cooked beets. Serve with buttered rye bread and a sweet and sour apple relish.

Serves 4

INGREDIENTS
2 eggs
8 pickled herrings
9 oz cooked baby beets
fresh flat-leaf parsley, to garnish
4 slices buttered rye bread, to serve

FOR THE RELISH
2 tbsp vegetable oil
2 large apples, peeled, cored and
    finely chopped
1 medium onion, chopped
1 tbsp sugar
1 tbsp cider vinegar
1 tsp hot mustard
pinch of salt

pickled herrings   *eggs*

baby beets

onion   *apples*

1 Bring a saucepan of water to a boil, gently lower in the eggs and cook for 10 minutes. Cool under running water and peel. Cut into quarters.

2 To make the relish, heat the oil in a saucepan and add the apple and onion. Cook over a gentle heat for 3–4 minutes without coloring. Add the sugar, vinegar and mustard, then season with salt.

3 Divide the herrings between four plates. Slice the beets and arrange to one side with the relish. Decorate with egg quarters and garnish with parsley. Serve with buttered rye bread, and a spoonful of sour cream if you wish.

COOK'S TIP

Choose full-flavored green or red apples for the best results.

Dover Sole in a Green Parsley Jacket

Quick to prepare and absolutely delicious, nothing compares with the rich sweetness of a Dover sole. Here, this fine fish sports a green parsley jacket trimmed with lemon and a hint of garlic.

Serves 2

INGREDIENTS
12 oz baking potatoes, peeled and
    finely chopped
1¼ cups milk, or as required
pinch of grated nutmeg
2 × Dover sole, skinned
2 tbsp butter
salt and freshly ground black pepper
lemon wedges, to serve

FOR THE PARSLEY JACKET
½ cup fresh parsley
1 oz crustless white bread, cubed
3 tbsp milk
2 tbsp olive oil
finely grated zest of ½ small lemon
1 small garlic clove, crushed

Dover sole

lemon

parsley

1 In a non-stick saucepan, cover the potatoes with the milk, add salt to taste, and the nutmeg, and bring to a boil. Simmer, uncovered, for 15 minutes until the potatoes have absorbed the milk. Mash, cover and keep warm.

2 To make the parsley jacket, chop the parsley in a food processor. Add the bread, milk, olive oil, lemon zest and garlic, then process to a fine paste.

3 Preheat a moderate broiler. Season the sole, dot with butter and broil for 5 minutes. Turn and allow 2 minutes on the other side. Spread with the parsley mixture, return to the broiler and continue to cook for a further 5 minutes. Serve with the mashed potatoes and wedges of lemon.

VARIATION

The same parsley mixture can be used to cover fillets of cod, haddock, whiting or flounder.

Herbed Fish Cakes with Lemon and Chive Sauce

The wonderful flavor of fresh herbs makes these fish cakes the catch of the day.

Serves 4

INGREDIENTS
12 oz potatoes, peeled
5 tbsp skimmed milk
12 oz haddock or flounder fillets, skinned
1 tbsp lemon juice
1 tbsp creamed horseradish
2 tbsp chopped fresh Italian parsley
flour, for dusting
2 cups fresh whole wheat bread crumbs
salt and freshly ground black pepper
sprig of Italian parsley, to garnish
snow peas and a sliced tomato and onion salad, to serve

FOR THE LEMON AND CHIVE SAUCE
thinly pared rind and juice of ½ small lemon
½ cup dry white wine
2 thin slices fresh ginger root
2 tsp cornstarch
2 tbsp snipped fresh chives

chives

potatoes

haddock

lemon

ginger

bread crumbs

parsley

1 Cook the potatoes in a large saucepan of boiling water for 15-20 minutes. Drain and mash with the milk and season to taste.

2 Purée the fish together with the lemon juice and horseradish in a blender or food processor. Mix together with the potatoes and parsley.

3 With floured hands, shape the mixture into eight fish cakes and coat with the bread crumbs. Chill in the refrigerator for 30 minutes.

4 Cook the fish cakes under a preheated moderate broiler for 5 minutes on each side, until browned.

5 To make the sauce, cut the lemon rind into julienne strips and put into a large saucepan together with the lemon juice, wine and ginger and season to taste.

6 Simmer uncovered for 6 minutes. Blend the cornstarch with 1 tbsp of cold water. Add to the saucepan and simmer until clear. Stir in the chives immediately before serving. Serve the sauce hot with the fish cakes, garnished with sprigs of Italian parsley and accompanied with snow peas and a sliced tomato and onion salad.

Butterfly Shrimp

Use raw shrimp if you can because the flavor will be better, but if you substitute cooked shrimp, cut down the stir-fry cooking time by one third.

Serves 4

INGREDIENTS
1 in piece ginger root
12 oz raw shrimp, thawed
    if frozen
½ cup raw peanuts, roughly
    chopped
3 tbsp vegetable oil
1 clove garlic, crushed
1 red chili, finely chopped
3 tbsp smooth peanut butter
1 tbsp fresh coriander, chopped
fresh coriander sprigs, to garnish

FOR THE DRESSING
⅔ cup natural low fat yogurt
2 in piece cucumber, diced
salt and freshly ground black pepper

1 To make the dressing, mix together the yogurt, cucumber and seasoning in a bowl, then leave to chill while preparing and cooking the shrimp.

2 Peel the ginger, and chop it finely.

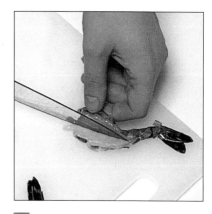

3 Prepare the shrimp by peeling off the shells, leaving the tails intact. Make a slit down the back of each shrimp and remove the black vein, then slit the shrimp completely down the back and open it out to make a "butterfly."

diced cucumber

peanuts

shrimp

coriander

chili

4 Heat the wok and dry-fry the peanuts, stirring constantly until golden brown. Leave to cool. Wipe out the wok with paper towels.

5 Heat the wok, add the oil and when hot add the ginger, garlic and chili. Stir-fry for 2–3 minutes until the garlic is softened but not brown.

6 Add the shrimp, then increase the heat and stir-fry for 1–2 minutes until the shrimp turn pink. Stir in the peanut butter and stir-fry for 2 minutes. Add the chopped coriander, then scatter in the peanuts. Garnish with coriander sprigs and serve with the cucumber dressing.

Cajun-style Cod

This recipe works equally well with any firm-fleshed fish such as swordfish, shark, tuna or halibut.

Serves 4

INGREDIENTS
4 cod steaks, each weighing
 about 6 oz
2 tbsp plain low fat yogurt
1 tbsp lime or lemon juice
1 garlic clove, crushed
1 tsp ground cumin
1 tsp paprika
1 tsp mustard powder
½ tsp cayenne pepper
½ tsp dried thyme
½ tsp dried oregano
baby potatoes and a mixed salad,
 to serve

cod

lime

mustard powder

thyme

paprika

1 Pat the fish dry on absorbent paper towels. Mix together the yogurt and lime or lemon juice and brush lightly over both sides of the fish.

2 Mix together the garlic clove, spices and herbs. Coat both sides of the fish with the seasoning mix, rubbing in well.

COOK'S TIP
If you don't have a ridged broiler pan, heat several metal skewers under a broiler until red hot. Holding the ends with a cloth, press onto the seasoned fish before cooking to give a seared appearance.

3 Spray a ridged broiler pan or heavy-based frying pan with non-stick cooking spray. Heat until very hot. Add the fish and cook over a high heat for 4 minutes, or until the underside is well browned.

4 Turn over and cook for a further 4 minutes, or until the steaks have cooked through. Serve immediately accompanied with baby potatoes and a mixed salad.

Sand Dab Provençal

Recreate the taste of the Mediterranean with this easy-to-make fish casserole.

Serves 4

INGREDIENTS
4 large sand dab fillets
2 small red onions
½ cup vegetable stock
4 tbsp dry red wine
1 garlic clove, crushed
2 zucchini, sliced
1 yellow bell pepper, seeded and
    sliced
14 oz can chopped tomatoes
1 tbsp chopped fresh thyme
salt and freshly ground black pepper

chopped tomatoes

plaice

thyme

zucchini

red onion   *bell pepper*

1 Preheat the oven to 350°F. Skin the sand dab fillets with a sharp knife by laying them skin-side down. Holding the tail end, push the knife between the skin and flesh in a sawing movement. Hold the knife at an angle with the blade towards the skin.

2 Cut each onion into eight wedges. Put into a heavy-based saucepan with the stock. Cover and simmer for 5 minutes. Uncover and continue to cook, stirring occasionally, until the stock has reduced entirely. Add the wine and garlic clove to the pan and continue to cook until the onions are soft.

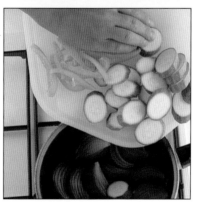

3 Add the zucchini, yellow pepper, tomatoes and thyme and season to taste. Simmer for 3 minutes. Spoon the sauce into a large casserole.

4 Fold each fillet in half and place on top of the sauce. Cover and cook in the preheated oven for 15-20 minutes until the fish is opaque and cooked.

Grilled Snapper with Hot Mango Salsa

A ripe mango provides the basis for a deliciously rich fruity salsa. The dressing needs no oil and features the tropical flavors of cilantro, ginger and chili.

VARIATION

If fresh mangoes are unavailable, use the canned variety and drain well. Sea bass are also good served with the hot mango salsa.

Serves 4

INGREDIENTS

12 oz new potatoes
3 eggs
4 oz green beans, topped, tailed and halved
4 × 12 oz red snapper, scaled and gutted
2 tbsp olive oil
6 oz mixed lettuce leaves, such as frisée or oak leaf
2 cherry tomatoes
salt and freshly ground black pepper

FOR THE SALSA

3 tbsp chopped fresh cilantro
1 medium sized ripe mango, peeled, pitted and diced
½ red chili, deseeded and chopped
1 in fresh ginger root, grated
juice of 2 limes
generous pinch of celery salt

1 Bring the potatoes to a boil in a large saucepan of salted water and simmer for 15–20 minutes. Drain.

2 Bring a second large saucepan of salted water to a boil. Put in the eggs and boil for 4 minutes, then add the beans and cook for a further 6 minutes, so that the eggs have had a total of 10 minutes. Remove the eggs from the pan, cool, peel and cut into quarters.

3 Preheat a moderate broiler. Slash each snapper three times on either side, moisten with oil and cook for 12 minutes, turning once.

4 To make the dressing, place the cilantro in a food processor. Add the mango, chili, ginger, lime juice and celery salt and process smoothly.

5 Moisten the lettuce leaves with olive oil, and distribute them between four large plates.

6 Arrange the snapper over the lettuce and season to taste. Halve the new potatoes and tomatoes, and distribute them with the beans and quartered hard-boiled eggs over the salad. Serve with the salsa dressing.

green beans

red snapper

mango

ginger

chili

Marinated Monkfish and Mussel Skewers

You can cook these fish kebabs on the barbecue – when the weather allows!

Serves 4

INGREDIENTS
1 lb monkfish, skinned and boned
1 tsp olive oil
2 tbsp lemon juice
1 tsp paprika
1 garlic clove, crushed
4 turkey bacon rashers
8 cooked mussels
8 raw shrimp
1 tbsp chopped fresh dill
salt and freshly ground black pepper
lemon wedges, to garnish
salad leaves and long-grain and wild rice, to serve

mussels   *turkey rashers*

dill

lemon

monkfish

1 Cut the monkfish into 1 in cubes and place in a shallow glass dish. Mix together the oil, lemon juice, paprika, and garlic clove and season with pepper.

2 Pour the marinade over the fish and toss to coat evenly. Cover and leave in a cool place for 30 minutes.

COOK'S TIP
Monkfish is ideal for kebabs, but can be expensive. Cod makes a good alternative.

3 Cut the turkey rashers in half and wrap each strip around a mussel. Thread onto skewers alternating with the fish cubes and raw shrimp.

4 Cook the kebabs under a hot broiler for 7-8 minutes, turning once and basting with the marinade. Sprinkle with chopped dill and salt. Garnish with lemon wedges and serve with salad and rice.

Pasta with Spinach and Anchovy Sauce

Deliciously earthy, this would make a good entree or light supper dish. Add golden raisins for something really special.

Serves 4

INGREDIENTS

2 lb fresh spinach or 1¼ lb frozen leaf spinach, thawed
1 lb angel hair pasta
salt
4 tbsp olive oil
3 tbsp pine nuts
2 garlic cloves, crushed
6 canned anchovy fillets or whole salted anchovies, drained and chopped
butter, for tossing the pasta

olive oil

pine nuts

spinach

anchovy fillets

garlic   *angel hair pasta*

1 Wash the spinach well and remove the tough stalks. Drain thoroughly. Place in a large saucepan with only the water that still clings to the leaves. Cover with a lid and cook over a high heat, shaking the pan occasionally, until the spinach is just wilted and still bright green. Drain.

2 Cook the pasta in plenty of boiling salted water according to the manufacturer's instructions.

3 Heat the oil in a saucepan and fry the pine nuts until golden. Remove with a perforated spoon. Add the garlic to the oil in the pan and fry until golden. Add the anchovies.

4 Stir in the spinach, and cook for 2–3 minutes or until heated through. Stir in the pine nuts. Drain the pasta, toss in a little butter, and transfer to a warmed serving bowl. Top with the sauce and fork through roughly.

Smoked Trout Cannelloni

Smoked trout can be bought already filleted or whole.
If you buy fillets, you'll need 8 oz of fish.

Serves 4–6

INGREDIENTS
1 large onion, finely chopped
1 garlic clove, crushed
4 tbsp vegetable stock
2 × 14 oz cans chopped tomatoes
½ tsp dried mixed herbs
1 smoked trout, weighing about
    14 oz
¾ cup frozen peas, thawed
1½ cups fresh bread crumbs
16 cannelloni tubes, cooked
salt and freshly ground black pepper
mixed salad, to serve

FOR THE CHEESE SAUCE
2 tbsp low fat spread
¼ cup flour
1½ cups skim milk
freshly grated nutmeg
1½ tbsp freshly grated Parmesan
    cheese

mixed herbs

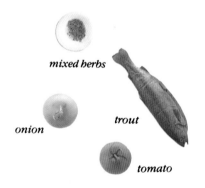
onion   *trout*

tomato

chopped tomatoes   *cannelloni*

1 Simmer the onion, garlic clove and stock in a large covered saucepan for 3 minutes. Uncover and continue to cook, stirring occasionally, until the stock has reduced entirely.

2 Stir in the tomatoes and dried herbs. Simmer uncovered for a further 10 minutes, or until very thick.

3 Meanwhile, skin the smoked trout with a sharp knife. Carefully flake the flesh and discard all the bones. Mix the fish together with the tomato mixture, peas, bread crumbs, salt and freshly ground black pepper.

4 Preheat the oven to 375°F. Spoon the filling into the cannelloni tubes and arrange in an ovenproof dish.

5 For the sauce, put the low fat spread, flour and milk into a saucepan and cook over a medium heat, whisking constantly until the sauce thickens. Simmer for 2-3 minutes, stirring all the time. Season to taste with salt, freshly ground black pepper and nutmeg.

COOK'S TIP

You can use a 7 oz can of tuna in water in place of the trout, if preferred.

6 Pour the sauce over the cannelloni and sprinkle with the grated Parmesan cheese. Bake in the preheated oven for 35-40 minutes, or until the top is golden and bubbling. Serve with a mixed salad.

Spaghetti with Tomato and Clam Sauce

Small sweet clams make this a delicately succulent sauce. Mussels would make a good substitute, but don't be tempted to use seafood pickled in vinegar – the result will be inedible!

Serves 4

INGREDIENTS
2 lb live small clams, or 2 × 14 oz
    cans clams in brine, drained
6 tbsp olive oil
2 garlic cloves, crushed
1 lb 5 oz canned chopped tomatoes
3 tbsp chopped fresh parsley
salt and pepper
1 lb spaghetti

spaghetti

olive oil

parsley

garlic

clams

1 If using live clams, place them in a bowl of cold water and rinse several times to remove any grit or sand. Drain.

2 Heat the oil in a saucepan and add the clams. Stir over a high heat until the clams open. Throw away any that do not open. Transfer the clams to a bowl with a perforated spoon.

3 Reduce the clam juice left in the pan to almost nothing by boiling fast; this will also concentrate the flavor. Add the garlic and fry until golden. Pour in the tomatoes, bring to a boil, and cook for 3–4 minutes until reduced. Stir in the clam mixture or canned clams, and half the parsley and heat through. Season.

4 Cook the pasta in plenty of boiling salted water according to the manufacturer's instructions. Drain well and transfer to a warm serving dish. Pour over the sauce and sprinkle with the remaining parsley.

Pasta with Tuna, Capers, and Anchovies

This piquant sauce could be made without the addition of tomatoes – just heat the oil, add the other ingredients, and heat through gently before tossing with the pasta.

Serves 4

INGREDIENTS
14 oz canned tuna fish in oil
2 tbsp olive oil
2 garlic cloves, crushed
1¾ lb canned chopped tomatoes
6 canned anchovy fillets, drained
2 tbsp capers in vinegar, drained
2 tbsp chopped fresh basil
salt and pepper
1 lb rigatoni, garganelle or penne
fresh basil sprigs, to garnish

olive oil

rigatoni

tuna fish

basil

anchovy fillets

capers

garlic

1 Drain the oil from the tuna into a saucepan, add the olive oil, and heat gently until it stops 'spitting'.

2 Add the garlic and fry until golden. Stir in the tomatoes and simmer for 25 minutes until thickened.

3 Flake the tuna and cut the anchovies in half. Stir into the sauce with the capers and chopped basil. Season well.

4 Cook the pasta in plenty of boiling salted water according to the manufacturer's instructions. Drain well and toss with the sauce. Garnish with fresh basil sprigs.

Seafood Pasta Shells with Spinach Sauce

You'll need very large pasta shells, measuring about 1½ in long for this dish; don't try stuffing smaller shells – it's much too fussy!

Serves 4

INGREDIENTS
1 tbsp low fat spread
8 scallions, finely sliced
6 tomatoes
32 large dried pasta shells
1 cup low fat cream cheese
6 tbsp skim milk
pinch of freshly grated nutmeg
8 oz shrimp
6 oz can white crabmeat, drained and flaked
4 oz frozen chopped spinach, thawed and drained
salt and freshly ground black pepper

scallions

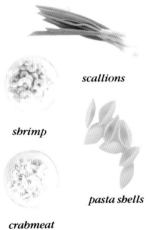
shrimp

pasta shells

crabmeat

spinach

tomatoes

1 Preheat the oven to 300°F. Melt the low fat spread in a small saucepan and gently cook the scallions for 3-4 minutes, or until softened.

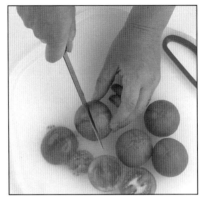

2 Plunge the tomatoes into a saucepan of boiling water for 1 minute, then into a saucepan of cold water. Slip off the skins. Halve the tomatoes, remove the seeds and cores and roughly chop the flesh.

3 Cook the pasta shells in lightly salted boiling water for about 10 minutes, or until *al dente*. Drain well.

4 Put the low fat cream cheese and skim milk into a saucepan and heat gently, stirring until blended. Season with salt, freshly ground black pepper and a pinch of nutmeg. Measure 2 tbsp of the sauce into a bowl.

5 Add the scallions, tomatoes, shrimp, and crabmeat to the bowl. Mix well. Spoon the filling into the shells and place in a single layer in a shallow ovenproof dish. Cover with foil and cook in the preheated oven for 10 minutes.

6 Stir the spinach into the remaining sauce. Bring to a boil and simmer gently for 1 minute, stirring all the time. Drizzle over the pasta shells and serve hot.

Grilled Salmon and Spring Vegetable Salad

Spring is the time to enjoy sweet young vegetables. Cook them briefly, cool to room temperature, dress, and serve with a piece of lightly grilled salmon topped with sorrel and quails' eggs.

Serves 4

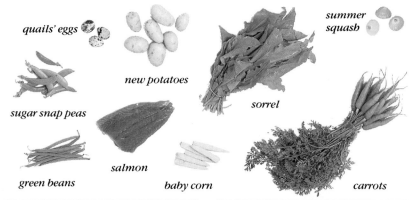

quails' eggs

summer squash

new potatoes

sorrel

sugar snap peas

salmon

green beans

baby corn

carrots

INGREDIENTS

12 oz small new potatoes, scrubbed or scraped
4 quails' eggs
4 oz young carrots, peeled
4 oz baby corn
4 oz sugar-snap peas, topped and tailed
4 oz fine green beans, topped and tailed
4 oz young zucchini
4 oz patty pan squash (optional)

½ cup French dressing
4 salmon fillets, each weighing 5 oz, skinned
4 oz sorrel or young spinach, stems removed
salt and freshly ground black pepper

1 Bring the potatoes to the boil in salted water and cook for 15–20 minutes. Drain, cover and keep warm.

2 Cover the quails' eggs with boiling water and cook for 8 minutes. Refresh under cold water, shell and cut in half.

3 Bring a saucepan of salted water to a the boil, add all the vegetables and cook for 2–3 minutes. Drain well. Place the hot vegetables and potatoes in a salad bowl, moisten with French dressing and allow to cool.

4 Brush the salmon fillets with French dressing and broil for 6 minutes, turning once.

5 Place the sorrel in a stainless-steel or enamel saucepan with 60 ml/2 tbsp French dressing, cover and soften over a gentle heat for 2 minutes. Strain in a small sieve and cool to room temperature.

6 Divide the potatoes and vegetables between 4 large plates, then position a piece of salmon in the centre of each. Finally place a spoonful of sorrel on each piece of salmon and top with a halved quails' egg. Season and serve at room temperature.

Avocado, Crab and Cilantro Salad

The sweet richness of crab combines especially well with ripe avocado, fresh cilantro and tomato.

Serves 4

INGREDIENTS
1½ lb small new potatoes
1 sprig fresh mint
2 lb boiled crabs, or 10 oz frozen crab
  meat
1 Batavian endive or butterhead
  lettuce
6 oz lamb's lettuce or young spinach
1 large ripe avocado, peeled and
  sliced
6 oz cherry tomatoes
salt, pepper and nutmeg

DRESSING
5 tbsp olive oil, preferably Tuscan
1 tbsp lime juice
3 tbsp chopped fresh cilantro
½ tsp superfine sugar

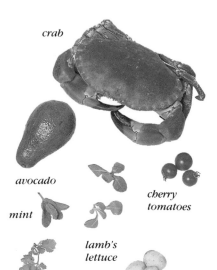

crab

avocado

mint

cherry tomatoes

lamb's lettuce

cilantro

new potatoes

1 Scrape or peel the potatoes. Cover with water, add a good pinch of salt, and a sprig of mint. Bring to a boil and simmer for 20 minutes. Drain, cover, and keep warm until needed.

2 Remove the legs and claws from each crab. Crack these open with the back of a chopping knife and then remove the white meat.

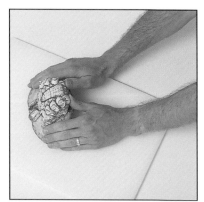

3 Turn the crab on its back and push the rear leg section away with the thumb and forefinger of each hand. Remove the flesh from inside the shell.

4 Discard the soft gills ('dead men's fingers'): the crab uses these gills to filter impurities in its diet. Apart from these and the shell, everything else is edible – white and dark meat.

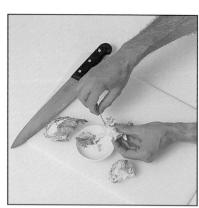

5 Split the central body section open with a knife and remove the white and dark flesh with a pick or skewer.

COOK'S TIP

Young crabs offer the sweetest meat, but are more fiddly to prepare than older, larger ones. The hen crab carries more flesh than the cock which is considered to have a better overall flavour. The cock crab, shown here, is identified by his narrow apron flap at the rear. The hen has a broad flap under which she carries her eggs. Frozen crab meat is a good alternative to fresh and retains much of its original sweetness.

6 Combine the dressing ingredients in a screw-top jar and shake. Wash and spin the lettuces, then dress them. Distribute between 4 plates. Top with avocado, crab, tomatoes and warm new potatoes. Season with salt, pepper and freshly grated nutmeg and serve.

Pasta, Melon and Shrimp Salad

Orange-fleshed cantaloupe or Charentais melon looks spectacular in this salad. You could also use a mixture of honeydew, cantaloupe and watermelon.

Serves 4–6

INGREDIENTS
1 ½ cups pasta shapes
½ lb frozen shrimp, thawed and
    drained
1 large or 2 small melons
4 tbsp olive oil
1 tbsp tarragon vinegar
2 tbsp chopped fresh chives or parsley
sprigs of herbs, to garnish
Napa cabbage, to serve

melons

pasta shapes

shrimp

Napa cabbage

1 Cook the pasta in boiling salted water according to the manufacturer's instructions. Drain well and allow to cool.

2 Peel the shrimp and discard the shells.

3 Halve the melon and remove the seeds with a teaspoon. Carefully scoop the flesh into balls with a melon baller and mix with the shrimp and pasta.

4 Whisk the oil, vinegar, and chopped herbs together. Pour on to the shrimp mixture and toss to coat. Cover and chill for at least 30 minutes.

5 Meanwhile shred the Napa cabbage and use to line a shallow bowl or the empty melon halves.

6 Pile the shrimp mixture onto the Napa cabbage and garnish with herbs.

Tuna Fish and Flageolet Bean Salad

Two cans of tuna fish form the basis of this delicious store cupboard salad.

Serves 4

INGREDIENTS
6 tbsp low fat mayonnaise
1 tsp mustard
2 tbsp capers
3 tbsp chopped fresh parsley
pinch of celery salt
2 × 7 oz cans tuna fish in oil,
 drained
3 Bibb lettuces
1 × 14 oz can flageolet beans,
 drained
1 × 14 oz can baby artichoke hearts,
 halved
12 cherry tomatoes, halved
toasted sesame bread, to serve

tomatoes

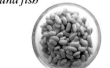
parsley

Bibb lettuce

artichoke hearts

mustard

capers

tuna fish

flageolet beans

1 Combine the mayonnaise, mustard, capers and parsley in a mixing bowl. Season to taste with celery salt. Flake the tuna into the dressing and toss gently.

2 Arrange the lettuce leaves on four plates, then spoon the tuna mixture onto the leaves.

VARIATION
Flageolet beans are taken from the under-developed pods of navy beans. They have a sweet creamy flavor and an attractive green color. If not available, use cannellini beans.

3 Spoon the flageolet beans to one side, followed by the tomatoes and artichoke hearts. Serve with slices of toasted sesame bread.

Smoked Trout and Horseradish Salad

Salads are the easy answer to fast, healthy eating. When lettuce is sweet and crisp, partner it with fillets of smoked trout, warm new potatoes and a creamy horseradish dressing.

Serves 4

INGREDIENTS
1½ lb new potatoes
4 smoked trout fillets
4 oz mixed lettuce leaves
4 slices dark rye bread, cut into
   fingers
salt and freshly ground black pepper

FOR THE DRESSING
4 tbsp creamed horseradish
4 tbsp groundnut oil
1 tbsp white wine vinegar
2 tsp caraway seeds

1 Bring the potatoes to a boil in a saucepan of salted water and simmer for 20 minutes. Remove the skin from the trout, and lift the flesh from the bone.

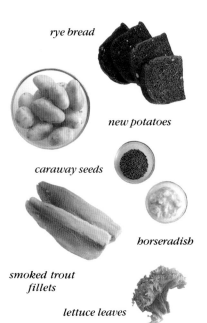

rye bread

new potatoes

caraway seeds

horseradish

smoked trout fillets

lettuce leaves

2 To make the dressing, place all the ingredients in a screw-topped jar and shake vigorously. Season the lettuce leaves and moisten them with the prepared dressing. Distribute between four plates.

3 Flake the trout fillets and halve the potatoes. Scatter them together with the rye fingers over the salad leaves and toss to mix. Season to taste and serve.

COOK'S TIP

To save time washing lettuce leaves, buy them ready-prepared from your supermarket. It is better to season the leaves rather than the dressing when making a salad.

Indonesian-style Satay Chicken

Use boneless chicken thighs to give a good flavor to these satays.

Serves 4

INGREDIENTS
½ cup raw peanuts
3 tbsp vegetable oil
1 small onion, finely chopped
1 in piece ginger root, peeled and finely chopped
1 clove garlic, crushed
1½ lb chicken thighs, skinned and cut into cubes
3½ oz creamed coconut, chopped
1 tbsp chili sauce
4 tbsp chunky peanut butter
1 tsp soft dark brown sugar
⅔ cup skim milk
¼ tsp salt

1 Shell and rub the skins from the peanuts, then soak them in enough water to cover for 1 minute. Drain the nuts and cut them into slivers.

2 Heat the wok and add 1 tsp oil. When the oil is hot, stir-fry the peanuts for 1 minute until crisp and golden. Remove with a slotted spoon and drain on paper towels.

3 Add the remaining oil to the hot wok. When the oil is hot, add the onion, ginger and garlic and stir-fry for 2–3 minutes until softened but not browned. Remove with a slotted spoon and drain on paper towels.

creamed coconut

peanuts

chili sauce

peanuts butter

4 Add the chicken pieces and stir-fry for 3–4 minutes until crisp and golden on all sides. Thread on to pre-soaked bamboo skewers and keep warm.

5 Add the creamed coconut to the hot wok in small pieces and stir-fry until melted. Add the chili sauce, peanut butter and cooked ginger and garlic, and simmer for 2 minutes. Stir in the sugar, milk and salt, and simmer for a further 3 minutes. Serve the skewered chicken hot, with a dish of the hot dipping sauce sprinkled with the roasted peanuts.

Chicken Teriyaki

A bowl of boiled rice is the ideal accompaniment to this Japanese-style chicken dish.

Serves 4

INGREDIENTS
1 lb boneless, skinless chicken breasts

FOR THE MARINADE
1 tsp sugar
1 tbsp sake or rice wine
1 tbsp rice wine or dry sherry
2 tbsp dark soy sauce
rind of 1 orange, grated
orange segments and cress,
    to garnish

orange

rice wine

soy sauce

chicken breast

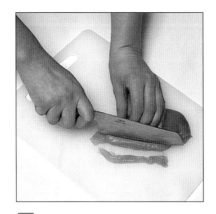

1 Finely slice the chicken.

2 Mix all the marinade ingredients together in a bowl.

COOK'S TIP
Make sure the marinade is brought to a boil and cooked for 4–5 minutes, because it has been in contact with raw chicken.

3 Place the chicken in a bowl, pour over the marinade and leave to marinate for 15 minutes.

4 Heat the wok, add the chicken and marinade and stir-fry for 4–5 minutes. Serve garnished with orange segments and cress.

Stir-fried Sweet and Sour Chicken

There are few cooking concepts that are better suited to today's busy lifestyle than the all-in-one stir-fry. This one has a South-east Asian influence.

Serves 4

INGREDIENTS

10 oz Chinese egg noodles
2 tbsp vegetable oil
3 scallions, chopped
1 garlic clove, crushed
1 in fresh ginger root, peeled and
    grated
1 tsp hot paprika
1 tsp ground coriander
3 boneless chicken breasts, sliced
1 cup sugar-snap peas, topped
    and tailed
4 oz baby corn, halved
8 oz fresh bean sprouts
1 tbsp cornstarch
3 tbsp soy sauce
3 tbsp lemon juice
1 tbsp sugar
3 tbsp chopped fresh cilantro or
    scallion tops, to garnish

COOK'S TIP

Large wok lids are cumbersome and can be difficult to store in a small kitchen. Consider placing a circle of waxed paper against the food surface to keep cooking juices in.

1 Bring a large saucepan of salted water to a boil. Add the noodles and cook according to the package instructions. Drain, cover and keep warm.

chicken breasts *garlic* *scallions*

paprika *egg noodles*

soy sauce *ginger*

sugar-snap peas

2 Heat the oil. Add the scallions and cook over a gentle heat. Mix in the next five ingredients, then stir-fry for 3–4 minutes. Add the next three ingredients and steam briefly. Add the noodles.

3 Combine the cornstarch, soy sauce, lemon juice and sugar in a small bowl. Add to the wok and simmer briefly to thicken. Serve garnished with chopped cilantro or scallion tops.

Lemon Chicken Stir-fry

It is essential to prepare all the ingredients before you begin so they are ready to cook. This dish is cooked in minutes.

Serves 4

INGREDIENTS
4 boned and skinned chicken breasts
1 tbsp light soy sauce
5 tbsp cornstarch
1 bunch scallions
1 lemon
1 garlic clove, crushed
1 tbsp superfine sugar
2 tbsp sherry
⅔ cup fresh or canned chicken stock
4 tbsp olive oil
salt and freshly ground black pepper

superfine sugar

garlic   *olive oil*

scallions

lemon

soy sauce

cornstarch

chicken breasts

1 Divide the chicken breasts into two natural fillets. Place each between two sheets of plastic wrap and flatten to a thickness of ¼ in with a rolling pin.

2 Cut into 1 in strips across the grain of the fillets. Put the chicken into a bowl with the soy sauce and toss to coat thoroughly, then sprinkle over 4 tbsp cornstarch to coat each piece.

3 Trim the roots off the scallions and cut diagonally into ½ in pieces. With a swivel peeler, remove the lemon rind in thin strips and cut into fine shreds. Reserve the lemon juice. Have ready the garlic clove, sugar, sherry, stock, lemon juice and the remaining cornstarch blended to a paste with cold water.

4 Heat the oil in a wok or large frying pan and cook the chicken very quickly in small batches for 3–4 minutes until lightly colored. Remove and keep warm while frying the rest of the chicken.

5 Add the scallions and garlic to the pan and cook for 2 minutes.

6 Add the remaining ingredients and bring to a boil, stirring until thickened. Add more sherry or stock if necessary and stir until the chicken is evenly covered with sauce. Reheat for 2 more minutes. Serve immediately.

Sweet and Sour Kebabs

This marinade contains sugar and will burn very easily, so grill the kebabs slowly, turning often. Serve with Harlequin Rice.

Serves 4

INGREDIENTS
2 boned and skinned chicken breasts
8 pickling onions or 2 medium
 onions, peeled
4 lean bacon rashers
3 firm bananas
1 red pepper, seeded and diced

FOR THE MARINADE
2 tbsp brown sugar
1 tbsp Worcestershire sauce
2 tbsp lemon juice
salt and freshly ground black pepper

FOR THE HARLEQUIN RICE
2 tbsp olive oil
generous 1 cup cooked rice
1 cup cooked peas
1 small red pepper, seeded and diced

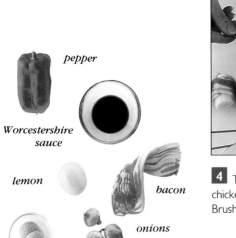

pepper

Worcestershire sauce

lemon

bacon

sugar

onions

bananas

chicken breast

1 Mix together the marinade ingredients. Cut each chicken breast into four pieces, add to the marinade, cover and leave for at least four hours or preferably overnight.

2 Peel the pickling onions, blanch them in boiling water for 5 minutes and drain. If using medium onions, quarter them after blanching.

3 Cut each rasher of bacon in half. Peel the bananas and cut each into three pieces. Wrap a rasher of bacon around each piece of banana.

4 Thread onto metal skewers with the chicken pieces, onions and pepper pieces. Brush with the marinade.

5 Broil or barbecue over low coals for 15 minutes, turning and basting frequently with the marinade. Keep warm while you prepare the rice.

COOK'S TIP
Pour boiling water over the small onions and then drain, to make peeling easier.

6 Heat the oil in a frying pan and add the rice, peas and diced pepper. Stir the mixture until heated through and serve with the kebabs.

Chicken Biriani

This is a good dish for entertaining. It can be prepared in advance and reheated in the oven. Serve with traditional curry accompaniments.

Serves 8

INGREDIENTS
2 lb boneless chicken thighs
4 tbsp olive oil
2 large onions, thinly sliced
1–2 green chilies, seeded and finely
   chopped
1 tsp grated fresh ginger root
1 garlic clove, crushed
1 tbsp hot curry powder
⅔ cup fresh or canned chicken stock
⅔ cup plain low fat yogurt
2 tbsp chopped fresh coriander
salt and freshly ground black pepper

FOR THE SPICED RICE
1 lb basmati rice
½ tsp garam masala
3¾ cups fresh or canned chicken
   stock or water
⅓ cup raisins or sultanas
¼ cup toasted almonds

ginger

basmati rice

curry powder

chilies

yogurt

coriander

chicken thighs

almonds

COOK'S TIP

Cover with buttered foil and bake in the oven for 30 minutes to reheat.

1 Put the basmati rice into a sieve and wash under cold running water to remove any starchy powder coating the grains. Then put into a bowl and cover with cold water and soak for 30 minutes. The grains will absorb some water so that they will not stick together in a solid mass while cooking.

2 Preheat the oven to 325°F. Cut the chicken into even-sized cubes, each approximately 1 in square. Heat half the oil in a large flameproof casserole, add one onion and cook until softened but not browned. Add the finely chopped chilies, ginger, garlic and curry powder and cook for a further 2 minutes, stirring occasionally.

3 Add the stock and seasoning, bring to a boil and add the chicken pieces. Cover and continue cooking in the oven for about 20 minutes or until tender.

4 Remove from the oven and then stir in the yogurt.

5 Meanwhile, heat the remaining oil in a flameproof casserole and cook the remaining onion gently until tender and lightly browned. Add the drained rice, garam masala and stock or water. Bring to a boil, cover and cook in the oven with the chicken for 25–35 minutes or until tender and the stock has been absorbed.

6 To serve, stir the raisins or sultanas and toasted almonds into the rice. Spoon half the rice into a large deep serving dish, cover with the chicken and then the remaining rice. Sprinkle with chopped coriander to garnish.

Hot and Sour Pork

Chinese five-spice powder is made from a mixture of ground star anise, Szechuan pepper, cassia, cloves and fennel seed and has a flavor similar to liquorice. If you can't find any, use mixed spice instead.

Serves 4

INGREDIENTS
12 oz pork fillet
1 tsp sunflower oil
1 in piece ginger root, grated
1 red chili, seeded and finely chopped
1 tsp Chinese five-spice powder
1 tbsp sherry vinegar
1 tbsp soy sauce
8 oz can pineapple chunks in natural juice
¾ cup chicken stock
4 tsp cornstarch
1 small green bell pepper, seeded and sliced
4 oz baby corn, halved
salt and freshly ground black pepper
sprig of Italian parsley, to garnish
boiled rice, to serve

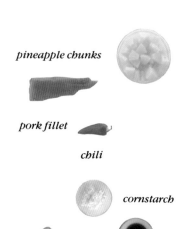

pineapple chunks

pork fillet

chili

cornstarch

soy sauce

bell pepper

baby corn

1 Preheat the oven to 325°F. Trim away any visible fat from the pork and cut into ½ in thick slices.

2 Brush the sunflower oil over the base of a flameproof casserole. Heat over a medium flame, then fry the meat for about 2 minutes on each side or until lightly browned.

3 Blend together the ginger, chili, five-spice powder, vinegar and soy sauce.

4 Drain the pineapple chunks, reserving the juice. Make the stock up to 1¼ cups with the reserved juice, mix together with the spices and pour over the pork.

5 Slowly bring to a boil. Blend the cornstarch with 1 tbsp of cold water and gradually stir into the pork. Add the vegetables and season to taste.

6 Cover and cook in the oven for 30 minutes. Stir in the pineapple and cook for a further 5 minutes. Garnish with Italian parsley and serve with boiled rice.

Honey-roast Pork with Thyme and Rosemary

Herbs and honey add flavor and sweetness to tenderloin – the leanest cut of pork.

Serves 4

INGREDIENTS
1 lb pork tenderloin
2 tbsp honey
2 tbsp Dijon mustard
1 tsp chopped fresh rosemary
½ tsp chopped fresh thyme
¼ tsp whole pink and green
    peppercorns
sprigs of fresh rosemary and thyme, to
    garnish

FOR THE RED ONION CONFIT
4 red onions
1½ cups vegetable stock
1 tbsp red wine vinegar
1 tbsp superfine sugar
1 garlic clove, crushed
2 tbsp ruby port
pinch of salt

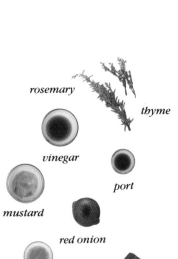

rosemary

thyme

vinegar

port

mustard

red onion

honey

pork

1 Preheat the oven to 350°F. Trim off any visible fat from the pork. Put the honey, mustard, rosemary and thyme in a small bowl and mix them together well.

2 Crush the peppercorns using a pestle and mortar. Spread the honey mixture over the pork and sprinkle with the crushed peppercorns. Place in a non-stick roasting pan and cook in the preheated oven for 35-45 minutes.

3 For the red onion confit, slice the onions into rings and put them into a heavy-based saucepan.

4 Add the stock, vinegar, sugar and garlic clove to the saucepan. Bring to a boil, then reduce the heat. Cover and simmer for 15 minutes.

5 Uncover and pour in the port and continue to simmer, stirring occasionally, until the onions are soft and the juices thick and syrupy. Season to taste with salt.

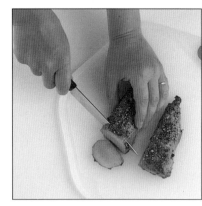

6 Cut the pork into slices and arrange on four warmed plates. Serve garnished with rosemary and thyme and accompanied with the red onion confit.

Lamb Tagine with Fruit

The slightly sharp taste of dried fruits complements the richness of lamb in this satisfying casserole.

Serves 4

INGREDIENTS
12 oz mixed dried fruit such
    as apple rings, apricots, pears
    and prunes
1½ lb boned lean lamb
1 onion, sliced
½ tsp ground ginger
1 tsp ground cilantro
large pinch of saffron strands
1 cinnamon stick
juice of 1 lemon
3⅔ cups vegetable
    stock
1 tsp chopped fresh thyme
1 tbsp honey
¼ cup blanched almonds, split and
    toasted, to garnish
sprig of fresh thyme, to garnish
steamed couscous, to serve

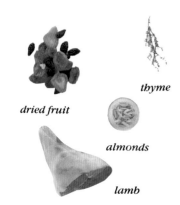

thyme

dried fruit

almonds

lamb

1 Rinse the dried fruit under cold running water. Put it into a large bowl and cover with plenty of cold water. Leave to soak for 4 hours.

2 Trim away any visible fat from the lamb and cut into 1 in cubes. Add it to a large, heavy-based saucepan together with the onion, spices, lemon juice and stock. Bring to a boil, and cover with a tight fitting lid. Simmer over a low heat for 2 hours.

3 Leave to cool, then chill in the refrigerator for at least 2 hours or until the fat solidifies on the top. Skim off the fat and discard.

4 Drain the fruit and add to the lamb together with the thyme and honey. Simmer uncovered for 15 minutes. Spoon into a warmed serving dish and garnish with toasted almonds and fresh thyme. Serve with steamed couscous.

Stir-fried Beef and Broccoli

This spicy beef may be served with noodles or on a bed of boiled rice for a speedy and low calorie Chinese meal.

Serves 4

INGREDIENTS

12 oz sirloin or lean London
    broil steak
1 tbsp cornstarch
1 tsp sesame oil
12 oz broccoli, cut into small
    florets
4 scallions, sliced on the diagonal
1 carrot, cut into matchstick strips
1 garlic clove, crushed
1 in piece ginger root, cut into very
    fine strips
½ cup low fat beef stock
2 tbsp soy sauce
2 tbsp dry sherry
2 tsp light brown sugar
scallion tassels, to garnish
noodles or rice, to serve

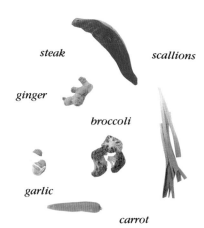

steak *scallions*

ginger

broccoli

garlic

carrot

1 Trim the beef and cut into thin slices across the grain. Cut each slice into thin strips. Toss in the cornstarch to coat thoroughly.

2 Heat the sesame oil in a large non-stick frying pan or wok. Add the beef strips and stir-fry over a brisk heat for 3 minutes. Remove and set aside.

COOK'S TIP

To make scallion tassels, trim the bulb base then cut the green shoot so that the onion is 3 in long. Shred to within 1 in of the base and put into iced water for 1 hour.

3 Add the broccoli, scallions, carrot, garlic clove, ginger and stock to the frying pan or wok. Cover and simmer for 3 minutes. Uncover and cook, stirring until all the stock has reduced entirely.

4 Mix the soy sauce, sherry and brown sugar together. Add to the frying pan or wok with the beef. Cook for 2–3 minutes stirring continuously. Spoon into a warm serving dish and garnish with scallion tassels. Serve on a bed of noodles or rice.

Burgundy Steak and Mushroom Pie

Tender chunks of beef are cooked in a rich wine sauce and a crisp filo pastry crust. It won't pile on the calories, although it may taste that way.

Serves 4

INGREDIENTS
1 onion, finely chopped
¾ cup low fat beef stock
1 lb lean sirloin or top round steak,
  cut into 1 in cubes
½ cup dry red wine
3 tbsp flour
8 oz button mushrooms, halved
5 sheets filo pastry
2 tsp sunflower oil
salt and freshly ground black pepper
mashed potatoes and wax beans,
  to serve

steak

onion

wine

flour

filo pastry

mushrooms

stock

1 Simmer the onion with ½ cup of the stock in a large covered non-stick saucepan for 5 minutes. Uncover and continue to cook, stirring occasionally, until the stock has reduced entirely. Transfer to a plate and set aside until required.

2 Add the steak to the saucepan and dry-fry until the meat is lightly browned. Return the onions to the saucepan together with the remaining stock and the red wine. Cover and simmer gently for about 1½ hours, or until tender.

3 Preheat the oven to 375°F. Blend the flour with 3 tbsp of cold water, add to the saucepan and simmer, stirring all the time until the sauce has thickened.

4 Add the mushrooms and continue to cook for 3 minutes. Season to taste and spoon into a 5 cup pie dish.

5 Brush a sheet of filo pastry with a little of the oil, then crumple it up loosely and place oil-side up over the filling. Repeat with the remaining pastry and oil.

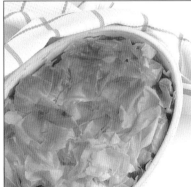

6 Bake in the oven for 25-30 minutes, until the pastry is golden brown and crispy. Serve with mashed potatoes and wax beans.

French Chicken Salad

A light first course for eight people or a substantial main course for four. Arrange attractively on individual plates to serve.

Serves 8

INGREDIENTS

1 × 3½ lb free-range chicken
1¼ cups white wine and water, mixed
24 × ¼ in slices French bread
1 garlic clove, peeled
8 oz green beans
4 oz fresh young spinach leaves
2 stalks celery, thinly sliced
2 scallions, thinly sliced
2 sun-dried tomatoes, chopped
fresh chives and parsley, to garnish

FOR THE VINAIGRETTE

2 tbsp red wine vinegar
6 tbsp olive oil
1 tbsp whole grain mustard
1 tbsp honey
2 tbsp chopped mixed fresh herbs, e.g. thyme, parsley and chives
2 tsp finely chopped capers
salt and freshly ground black pepper

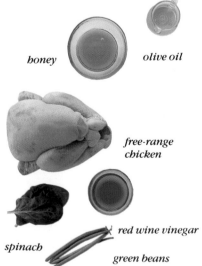

honey

olive oil

free-range chicken

spinach

red wine vinegar

green beans

1 Preheat the oven to 375°F. Put the chicken into a casserole with the wine and water. Roast for 1½ hours until tender. Leave to cool in the liquid. Remove the skin and bones and cut the flesh into small pieces.

2 To make the vinaigrette, put all the ingredients into a screw-topped jar and shake vigorously to emulsify. Adjust the seasoning to taste.

3 Toast the French bread under the broiler or in the oven until dry and golden brown, then lightly rub with the peeled garlic clove.

4 Trim the green beans, cut into 2 in lengths and cook in boiling water until just tender (*al dente*). Drain and rinse under cold running water.

5 Wash the spinach thoroughly, remove the stalks and tear into small pieces. Arrange on serving plates with the sliced celery, green beans, scallions, chicken and sun-dried tomatoes.

6 Spoon over the vinaigrette dressing. Arrange the toasted croûtons on top, garnish with extra fresh chives and parsley, if desired, and serve immediately.

Dijon Chicken Salad

An attractive and elegant dish to serve for lunch
with herb and garlic bread.

Serves 4

INGREDIENTS
4 boned and skinned chicken breasts
mixed salad leaves, e.g. watercress
  and oakleaf lettuce, to serve

FOR THE MARINADE
2 tbsp Dijon mustard
3 garlic cloves, crushed
1 tbsp grated onion
4 tbsp white wine

FOR THE MUSTARD DRESSING
2 tbsp tarragon wine vinegar
1 tsp Dijon mustard
1 tsp honey
6 tbsp olive oil
salt and freshly ground black pepper

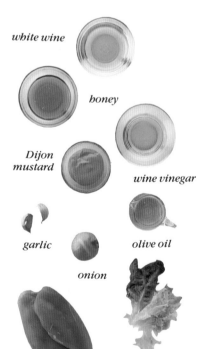

white wine

honey

Dijon
mustard

wine vinegar

garlic

olive oil

onion

salad leaves

chicken breasts

1 Mix all the marinade ingredients together in a shallow glass or earthenware dish that is large enough to hold the chicken in a single layer.

2 Turn the chicken over in the marinade to coat completely, cover with plastic wrap and then chill in the refrigerator overnight.

3 Preheat the oven to 375°F. Transfer the chicken and the marinade into an ovenproof dish, cover with foil and bake for about 35 minutes or until tender. Leave to cool in the liquid.

4 Put all the mustard dressing ingredients into a screw-topped jar, shake vigorously to emulsify, and adjust the seasoning. (This can be made several days in advance and stored in the refrigerator.)

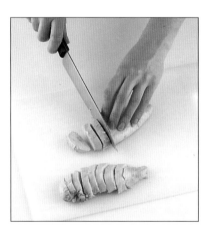

5 Slice the chicken thinly, fan out the slices and arrange on a serving dish with the salad leaves.

6 Spoon over some of the mustard dressing and serve.

Maryland Salad

Barbecue-grilled chicken, corn, bacon, banana and watercress combine here in a sensational main-course salad. Serve with baked potatoes and a knob of butter.

Serves 4

INGREDIENTS
4 boneless free-range chicken breasts
8 oz rindless unsmoked bacon
4 corn cobs
3 tbsp soft butter
4 ripe bananas, peeled and halved
4 firm tomatoes, halved
1 escarole or butterhead lettuce
1 bunch watercress
salt and freshly ground black pepper

DRESSING
5 tbsp groundnut oil
1 tbsp white wine vinegar
2 tsp maple syrup
2 tsp mild mustard

1 Season the chicken breasts, brush with oil and barbecue or broil for 15 minutes, turning once. Barbecue or grill the bacon for 8–10 minutes or until crisp.

2 Bring a large saucepan of salted water to the boil. Shuck and trim the corn cobs or leave the husks on if you prefer. Boil for 20 minutes. For extra flavour, brush with butter and brown over the barbecue or under the grill. Barbecue or grill the bananas and tomatoes for 6–8 minutes: you can brush these with butter too if you wish.

3 To make the dressing, combine the oil, vinegar, maple syrup and mustard with 1 tbsp water in a screw-top jar and shake well.

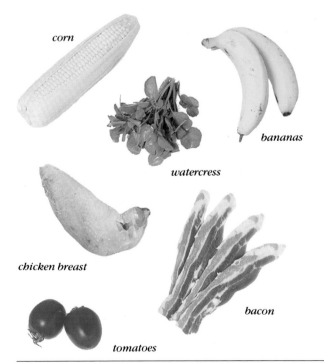

corn

bananas

watercress

chicken breast

bacon

tomatoes

4 Wash, spin thoroughly and dress the salad leaves.

5 Distribute the salad leaves between 4 large plates. Slice the chicken and arrange over the leaves with the bacon, banana, corn and tomatoes.

Warm Stir-fried Salad

Warm salads are becoming increasingly popular
because they are delicious and nutritious. Arrange the
salad leaves on four individual plates, so the hot
stir-fry can be served quickly on to them, ensuring the
lettuce remains crisp and the chicken warm.

Serves 4

INGREDIENTS

1 tbsp fresh tarragon

2 boneless, skinless chicken breasts,
   about 8 oz each

2 in piece ginger root, peeled and
   finely chopped

3 tbsp light soy sauce

1 tbsp sugar

1 tbsp sunflower oil

1 Napa cabbage

½ chicory lettuce, torn into bite-size
   pieces

1 cup unsalted cashews

2 large carrots, peeled and cut into
   fine strips

salt and freshly ground black pepper

chicken breast

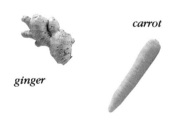

carrot

ginger

cashews

1 Chop the tarragon.

2 Cut the chicken into fine strips and place in a bowl.

3 To make the marinade, mix together in a bowl the tarragon, ginger, soy sauce, sugar and seasoning.

4 Pour the marinade over the chicken strips and leave for 2–4 hours.

5 Strain the chicken from the marinade. Heat the wok, then add the oil. When the oil is hot, stir-fry the chicken for 3 minutes, add the marinade and bubble for 2–3 minutes.

6 Slice the Napa cabbage and arrange on a plate with the chicory. Toss the cashews and carrots together with the chicken, pile on top of the bed of lettuce and serve immediately.

Sweet Potato Roulade

Sweet potato works particularly well as the base for this roulade. Serve in thin slices for a truly impressive dinner party dish.

Serves 6

INGREDIENTS
1 cup low fat ricotta cheese
5 tbsp low fat yogurt
6–8 scallions, finely sliced
2 tbsp chopped brazil nuts, roasted
1 lb sweet potatoes, peeled and
    coarsely cubed
12 allspice berries, crushed
4 eggs, separated
¼ cup Edam or Gouda cheese, finely
    grated
salt and freshly ground black pepper
1 tbsp sesame seeds

yogurt

sesame
seeds

sweet potato

ricotta cheese

Edam

brazil nuts

scallions

peppercorns

egg

1 Preheat the oven to 400°F. Grease and line a 13 × 10 in jelly roll pan with parchment paper, snipping the corners with scissors to fit neatly into the pan.

2 In a small bowl, mix together the ricotta, yogurt, scallions and brazil nuts. Set aside.

3 Boil or steam the sweet potato until tender. Drain well. Place in a food processor with the allspice and blend until smooth. Spoon into a bowl and stir in the egg yolks and Edam. Season to taste.

4 Whisk the egg whites until stiff but not dry. Fold ⅓ of the egg whites into the sweet potatoes to lighten the mixture before gently folding in the rest.

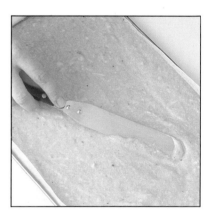

5 Pour into the prepared pan, tipping it to get the mixture right into the corners. Smooth gently with a spatula and cook in the oven for 10–15 minutes.

COOK'S TIP
Choose the orange-fleshed variety of sweet potato for the most striking color.

6 Meanwhile, lay a large sheet of waxed paper on a clean dish-towel and sprinkle with the sesame seeds. When the roulade is cooked, tip it onto the paper, trim the edges and roll it up. Leave to cool. When cool carefully unroll, spread with the filling and roll up again. Cut into slices to serve.

Ratatouille Crepes

These crepes are made slightly thicker than usual to hold the juicy vegetable filling.

Serves 4

INGREDIENTS
¾ cup flour
¼ cup oatmeal
1 egg
1¼ cups skim milk
mixed salad, to serve

FOR THE FILLING
1 large eggplant, cut into 1 in cubes
1 garlic clove, crushed
2 medium zucchini, sliced
1 green bell pepper, seeded and sliced
1 red bell pepper, seeded and sliced
5 tbsp vegetable stock
7 oz can chopped tomatoes
1 tsp cornstarch
salt and freshly ground black pepper

zucchini

oatmeal

pepper

cornstarch

chopped tomatoes

eggplant

flour

egg

1 Sift the flour and a pinch of salt into a bowl. Stir in the oatmeal. Make a well in the center, add the egg and half the milk and mix to a smooth batter. Gradually beat in the remaining milk. Cover the bowl and leave to stand for 30 minutes.

2 Spray a 7 in crepe pan or heavy-based frying pan with non-stick cooking spray. Heat the pan, then pour in just enough batter to cover the base of the pan thinly. Cook for 2-3 minutes, until the underside is golden brown. Flip over and cook for a further 1-2 minutes.

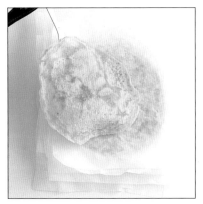

3 Slide the crepe out onto a plate lined with non-stick baking paper. Stack the other crepes on top as they are made, interleaving each with non-stick baking paper. Keep warm.

4 For the filling, put the eggplant in a colander and sprinkle well with salt. Leave to stand on a plate for 30 minutes. Rinse thoroughly and drain well.

5 Put the garlic clove, zucchini, peppers, stock and tomatoes into a large saucepan. Simmer uncovered and stir occasionally for 10 minutes. Add the eggplant and cook for a further 15 minutes. Blend the cornstarch with 2 tsp water and add to the saucepan. Simmer for 2 minutes. Season to taste.

6 Spoon the ratatouille mixture into the middle of each crepe. Fold each one in half, then in half again to make a cone shape. Serve hot with a mixed salad.

Paglia e Fieno

The title of this dish translates as 'straw and hay', which refers to the yellow and green colors of the pasta when mixed together. Using fresh peas makes all the difference to this dish.

Serves 4

INGREDIENTS
4 tbsp butter
2 cups frozen petits pois (small peas) or 2 lb fresh peas, shelled
⅔ cup heavy cream, plus 4 tbsp extra
1 lb tagliatelle (plain and spinach, mixed)
½ cup freshly grated Parmesan cheese, plus extra to serve
salt and pepper
freshly grated nutmeg

tagliatelle

peas

Parmesan cheese

COOK'S TIP
Sautéed mushrooms and narrow strips of cooked ham also make a good addition.

1 Melt the butter in a heavy saucepan and add the peas. Sauté for 2–3 minutes, then add the cream, bring to a boil, and simmer for 1 minute until slightly thickened.

2 Cook the fettuccine in plenty of boiling salted water according to the manufacturer's instructions, but for 2 minutes' less time. The pasta should still be *al dente*. Drain very well and transfer to the pan with the cream and pea sauce.

3 Place on the heat and toss the pasta in the sauce to coat. Pour in the extra cream, the cheese, salt and pepper to taste, and a little grated nutmeg. Toss until well coated and heated through. Serve immediately with extra Parmesan cheese.

Pasta Napoletana

The simple classic cooked tomato sauce with no adornments!

Serves 4

INGREDIENTS
2 lb fresh ripe red tomatoes or 1¾ lb
  canned plum tomatoes with juice
1 medium onion, chopped
1 medium carrot, diced
1 celery stick, diced
⅔ cup dry white wine (optional)
1 sprig fresh parsley
salt and pepper
pinch of superfine sugar
1 tbsp chopped fresh oregano or 1 tsp
  dried oregano
1 lb pasta, any variety
freshly grated Parmesan cheese, to
  serve

pasta

onion

tomatoes

celery

parsley

carrot

Parmesan cheese

1 Roughly chop the tomatoes and place in a medium saucepan.

2 Put all the ingredients – except the oregano, pasta, and cheese – into the pan with the tomatoes. Bring to a boil and simmer, half-covered, for 45 minutes until very thick, stirring occasionally. Pass through a strainer or liquidize and strain to remove the tomato seeds, then stir in the oregano. Taste to check the seasoning and adjust if necessary.

3 Cook the pasta in plenty of boiling salted water according to the manufacturer's instructions. Drain well.

4 Toss the pasta with the sauce. Serve with grated Parmesan cheese.

Spanish Omelet

Spanish omelet belongs in every cook's repertoire and can vary according to what you have in store. This version includes white beans and is finished with a layer of toasted sesame seeds.

Serves 4

INGREDIENTS
2 tbsp olive oil
1 tsp sesame oil
1 Spanish onion, chopped
1 small red bell pepper, seeded and
    diced
2 celery stalks, chopped
1 × 14 oz can soft white beans,
    drained
8 eggs
3 tbsp sesame seeds
salt and freshly ground black pepper
4 oz green salad, to serve

celery

red bell pepper

white beans

sesame oil

sesame seeds

eggs

VARIATION
You can also use sliced cooked potatoes, any seasonal vegetables, baby artichoke hearts and chick-peas in a Spanish omelet.

1 Heat the olive and sesame oils in a 12 in paella or frying pan. Add the onion, pepper and celery and cook to soften without coloring.

2 Add the beans and continue to cook for several minutes to heat through.

3 In a small bowl beat the eggs with a fork, season well and pour over the ingredients in the pan.

4 Stir the egg mixture with a flat wooden spoon until it begins to stiffen, then allow to firm over a low heat for about 6–8 minutes.

5 Preheat a moderate broiler. Sprinkle the omelette with sesame seeds and brown evenly under the broiler.

6 Cut the omelet into thick wedges and serve warm with a green salad.

Carrot Mousse with Mushroom Sauce

The combination of fresh vegetables in this impressive yet easy-to-make mousse make healthy eating a pleasure.

Serves 4

INGREDIENTS
12 oz carrots, roughly chopped
1 small red bell pepper, seeded and
 roughly chopped
3 tbsp vegetable stock or water
2 eggs
1 egg white
½ cup Quark or low fat soft cheese
1 tbsp chopped fresh tarragon
salt and freshly ground black pepper
sprig of fresh tarragon, to garnish
boiled rice and leeks, to serve

FOR THE MUSHROOM SAUCE
2 tbsp low fat spread
6 oz mushrooms, sliced
2 tbsp flour
1 cup skim milk

carrots
egg white
mushrooms
pepper
eggs
flour
cream cheese
low fat spread

1 Preheat the oven to 375°F. Line the bases of four ⅔ cup ramekin dishes with non-stick baking paper. Put the carrots and red pepper in a small saucepan with the vegetable stock or water. Cover and cook for 5 minutes, or until tender. Drain well.

2 Lightly beat the eggs and egg white together. Mix with the Quark or low fat cream cheese. Season to taste. Purée the cooked vegetables in a food processor or blender. Add the cheese mixture and process for a few seconds more until smooth. Stir in the chopped tarragon.

3 Divide the carrot mixture between the prepared ramekin dishes and cover with foil. Place the dishes in a roasting pan half-filled with hot water. Bake in the oven for 35 minutes, or until set.

4 For the mushroom sauce, melt 1 tbsp of the low fat spread in a frying pan. Add the mushrooms and gently sauté for 5 minutes, until soft.

5 Put the remaining low fat spread in a small saucepan together with the flour and milk. Cook over medium heat, stirring all the time, until the sauce thickens. Stir in the mushrooms and season to taste.

6 Turn out each mousse onto a serving plate. Spoon over a little sauce and serve the remainder separately. Garnish with a sprig of fresh tarragon and serve with boiled rice and leeks.

Tagliatelle with Walnut Sauce

An unusual sauce that would make this a spectacular dinner party starter.

Serves 4–6

INGREDIENTS
2 thick slices whole-wheat bread
1¼ cups milk
2½ cups walnut pieces
1 garlic clove, crushed
½ cup freshly grated Parmesan
   cheese
6 tbsp olive oil, plus extra for tossing
   the pasta
salt and pepper
1 lb tagliatelle
2 tbsp chopped fresh parsley

1 Cut the crusts off the bread and soak in the milk until the milk is all absorbed.

2 Preheat the oven to 375°F. Spread the walnuts on a baking sheet and toast in the oven for 5 minutes. Leave to cool.

3 Place the bread, walnuts, garlic, Parmesan cheese, and olive oil in a food processor and blend until smooth. Season to taste with salt and pepper.

tagliatelle

parsley

garlic

walnut pieces

4 Cook the pasta in plenty of boiling salted water, drain, and toss with a little olive oil. Divide the pasta equally between 4 bowls and place a dollop of sauce on each portion. Sprinkle liberally with parsley.

VARIATION

Add ¾ cup pitted black olives to the food processor with the other ingredients for a richer, more piquant sauce. The Greek-style olives have the most flavor.

Stir-fried Vegetables with Pasta

This is a colorful Chinese-style dish, easily prepared using pasta instead of Chinese noodles.

Serves 4

INGREDIENTS
1 medium carrot
6 oz small zucchini
6 oz green beans
6 oz baby corn
1 lb ribbon pasta such as tagliatelle
salt
2 tbsp corn oil, plus extra for tossing the pasta
½ in piece fresh ginger, peeled and finely chopped
2 garlic cloves, finely chopped
6 tbsp yellow bean sauce
6 scallions, sliced into 1 in lengths
2 tbsp dry sherry
1 tsp sesame seeds

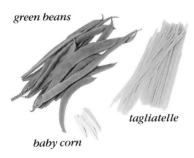

green beans

tagliatelle

baby corn

ginger

scallions

garlic

zucchini

1 Slice the carrot and zucchini diagonally into chunks. Slice the beans diagonally. Cut the baby corn diagonally in half.

2 Cook the pasta in plenty of boiling salted water according to the manufacturer's instructions, drain, then rinse under hot water. Toss in a little oil.

3 Heat 2 tbsp oil until smoking in a wok or skillet and add the ginger and garlic. Stir-fry for 30 seconds, then add the carrots, beans, and zucchini.

4 Stir-fry for 3–4 minutes, then stir in the yellow bean sauce. Stir-fry for 2 minutes, add the scallions, sherry, and pasta and stir-fry for 1 minute more until piping hot. Sprinkle with sesame seeds and serve immediately.

Pasta Tossed with Broiled Vegetables

A hearty dish to be eaten with crusty bread and washed down with a robust red wine. Try barbecuing the vegetables for a really smoky flavor.

Serves 4

INGREDIENTS
1 medium eggplant
2 medium zucchini
1 medium red bell pepper
8 garlic cloves, unpeeled
about ⅔ cup good olive oil
salt and pepper
1 lb ribbon pasta (pappardelle)
few sprigs fresh thyme, to garnish

olive oil

zucchini

eggplant

ribbon pasta

thyme

garlic

pepper

1 Preheat the broiler. Slice the eggplant and zucchini lengthwise.

2 Halve the bell pepper, cut out the stalk and white pith, and scrape out the seeds. Slice lengthwise into 8 pieces.

3 Line a broiler pan with foil and arrange the vegetables and unpeeled garlic in a single layer on top. Brush liberally with oil and season well with salt and pepper.

4 Grill until slightly charred, turning once. If necessary, cook the vegetables in 2 batches.

5 Cool the garlic, remove the charred skins, and halve. Toss the vegetables with olive oil and keep warm.

6 Meanwhile, cook the pasta in plenty of boiling salted water according to the manufacturer's instructions. Drain well and toss with the grilled vegetables. Serve immediately, garnished with sprigs of thyme and accompanied by plenty of country bread.

Sesame Noodle Salad with Hot Peanuts

An Orient-inspired salad with crunchy vegetables a light soy dressing. The hot peanuts make a surprisingly successful union with the cold noodles.

Serves 4

INGREDIENTS
12 oz egg noodles
2 carrots, peeled and cut into fine
    julienne strips
½ cucumber, peeled and cut into
    ½ in cubes
4 oz celeriac, peeled and cut into fine
    julienne strips
6 scallions, finely sliced
8 canned water chestnuts, drained
    and finely sliced
6 oz beansprouts
1 small fresh green chili, seeded and
    finely chopped
2 tbsp sesame seeds, to serve
1 cup peanuts, to serve

FOR THE DRESSING
1 tbsp dark soy sauce
1 tbsp light soy sauce
1 tbsp honey
1 tbsp rice wine or dry sherry
1 tbsp sesame oil

1 Preheat the oven to 400°F. Cook the egg noodles in boiling water, following the instructions on the side of the package.

2 Drain the noodles, refresh in cold water, then drain again.

3 Mix the noodles with all of the prepared vegetables.

celeriac

beansprouts

green chili

scallion

sesame seeds

water chestnuts

cucumber

peanuts

carrot

noodles

4 Combine the dressing ingredients in a small bowl, then toss into the noodle and vegetable mixture. Divide the salad between 4 plates.

5 Place the sesame seeds and peanuts on separate cookie sheets and place in the oven. Take the sesame seeds out after 5 minutes and continue to cook the peanuts for a further 5 minutes until evenly browned.

6 Sprinkle the sesame seeds and peanuts evenly over each portion and serve at once.

Cilantro Ravioli with Pumpkin filling

A stunning herb pasta with a superb creamy pumpkin and roast garlic filling.

Serves 4–6

INGREDIENTS
scant 1 cup flour
2 eggs
pinch of salt
3 tbsp chopped fresh cilantro
cilantro sprigs, to garnish

FOR THE FILLING
4 garlic cloves in their skins
1 lb pumpkin, peeled and seeds
    removed
½ cup ricotta cheese
4 halves sun-dried tomatoes in olive
    oil, drained and finely chopped, but
    reserve 2 tbsp of the oil
freshly ground black pepper

cilantro

pumpkin

egg

garlic

flour

ricotta
cheese

sun-dried tomatoes

1 Place the flour, eggs, salt and coriander into a food processor. Pulse until combined.

2 Place the dough on a lightly floured board and knead well for 5 minutes, until smooth. Wrap in plastic wrap and leave to rest in the fridge for 20 minutes.

3 Preheat the oven to 400°F. Place the garlic cloves on a cookie sheet and bake for 10 minutes until softened. Steam the pumpkin for 5–8 minutes until tender and drain well. Peel the garlic cloves and mash into the pumpkin together with the ricotta and drained sun-dried tomatoes. Season with black pepper.

4 Divide the pasta into 4 pieces and flatten slightly. Using a pasta machine, on its thinnest setting, roll out each piece. Leave the sheets of pasta on a clean dish-towel until slightly dried.

5 Using a 3 in crinkle-edged round cutter, stamp out 36 rounds.

6 Top 18 of the rounds with a teaspoonful of mixture, brush the edges with water and place another round of pasta on top. Press firmly around the edges to seal. Bring a large pan of water to a boil, add the ravioli and cook for 3–4 minutes. Drain well and toss into the reserved tomato oil. Serve garnished with coriander sprigs.

Spinach and Potato Galette

Creamy layers of potato, spinach and herbs make a warming supper dish.

Serves 6

INGREDIENTS
2 lb large potatoes
1 lb fresh spinach
2 eggs
14 oz (1¾ cups) low fat cream
   cheese
1 tbsp grainy mustard
3 tbsp chopped fresh herbs (e.g.
   chives, parsley, chervil or sorrel)
salt and freshly ground black pepper

mustard

parsley

cream cheese

spinach

egg

potatoes

chives

chervil

sorrel

1 Preheat the oven to 350°F. Line a deep 9 in cake pan with parchment paper. Place the potatoes in a large pot and cover with cold water. Bring to a boil and cook for 10 minutes. Drain well and allow to cool slightly before peeling and slicing thinly.

2 Wash the spinach well and place in a large pot with only the water that is clinging to the leaves. Cover and cook, stirring once, until the spinach has just wilted. Drain well in a sieve and squeeze out the excess moisture. Chop finely.

3 Beat the eggs with the cream cheese and mustard then stir in the chopped spinach and fresh herbs.

4 Place a layer of the sliced potatoes in the lined pan, arranging them in concentric circles. Top with a spoonful of the cream cheese mixture and spread out. Continue layering, seasoning with salt and pepper as you go, until all the potatoes and the cream cheese mixture are used up.

5 Cover the pan with a piece of foil and place in a roasting pan.

6 Fill the roasting pan with enough boiling water to come halfway up the sides, and cook in the oven for 45–50 minutes. Turn out onto a plate and serve hot or cold.

COOK'S TIP
Choose firm white or red skinned boiling potatoes for this dish.

Spiced Vegetables with Coconut

This spicy and substantial dish could be served as a starter, or as a vegetarian main course for two. Eat it with spoons and forks, and hunks of granary bread for mopping up the delicious coconut milk.

Serves 2–4

INGREDIENTS
1 red chili
2 large carrots
6 stalks celery
1 bulb fennel
2 tbsp grapeseed oil
1 in piece ginger root, peeled
  and grated
1 clove garlic, crushed
3 scallions, sliced
1 × 14 fl oz can thin coconut milk
1 tbsp fresh coriander, chopped
salt and freshly ground black pepper
coriander sprigs, to garnish

celery

scallions

fennel

carrot

1 Halve, dessed and finely chop the chili. If necessary, wear rubber gloves to protect your hands.

2 Slice the carrots on the diagonal. Slice the celery stalks on the diagonal.

3 Trim the fennel head and slice roughly, using a sharp knife.

4 Heat the wok, then add the oil. When the oil is hot, add the ginger and garlic, chili, carrots, celery, fennel and scallions and stir-fry for 2 minutes.

5 Stir in the coconut milk with a large spoon and bring to a boil.

6 Stir in the coriander and salt and pepper, and serve garnished with coriander sprigs.

Mixed Roasted Vegetables

Frying Parmesan cheese in this unusual way gives a wonderful crusty coating to the vegetables and creates a truly Mediterranean flavor.

Serves 4

INGREDIENTS
1 large eggplant, about 8 oz
salt, for sprinkling
6 oz plum tomatoes
2 red peppers
1 yellow pepper
2 tbsp olive oil
1 oz Parmesan cheese
2 tbsp fresh parsley, chopped
freshly ground black pepper

peppers

plum tomatoes

eggplant

1 Cut the eggplant into segments lengthwise. Place in a colander and sprinkle with salt. Leave for 30 minutes, to allow the salt to draw out the bitter juices.

2 Rinse off the salt under cold water and pat dry on paper towels.

3 Cut the plum tomatoes into segments lengthwise.

4 Cut the red and yellow peppers into quarters lengthwise and deseed.

5 Heat the wok, then add 1 tsp of the olive oil. When the oil is hot, add the Parmesan and stir-fry until golden brown. Remove from the wok, allow to cool and chop into fine flakes.

6 Heat the wok, and then add the remaining oil. When the oil is hot stir-fry the eggplant and peppers for 4–5 minutes. Stir in the tomatoes and stir-fry for a further 1 minute. Toss the vegetables in the Parmesan, parsley and black pepper and serve.

Baked Squash

A creamy, sweet and nutty filling makes the perfect topping for tender buttery squash.

Serves 4

INGREDIENTS

2 butternut or acorn squash, 1 ¼ lb
  each
1 tbsp olive oil
¾ cup canned corn kernels, drained
½ cup unsweetened chestnut purée
5 tbsp low fat yogurt
salt and freshly ground black pepper
¼ cup fresh goat cheese
snipped chives, to garnish

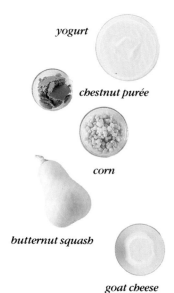

yogurt

chestnut purée

corn

butternut squash

goat cheese

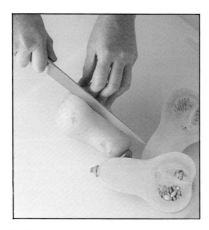

1 Preheat the oven to 350°F. Cut the squash in half lengthwise.

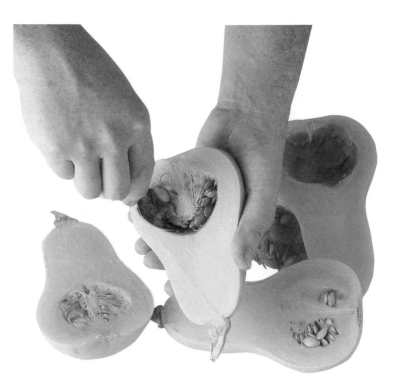

2 Scoop out the seeds with a spoon and discard.

3 Place the squash halves on a cookie sheet and brush the flesh lightly with the oil. Bake in the oven for 30 minutes.

4 Mix together the corn, chestnut purée and yogurt in a bowl. Season to taste.

5 Remove the squash from the oven and divide the chestnut mixture between them, spooning it into the hollows.

Cook's Tip
Use mozzarella or other mild, soft cheeses in place of goat cheese. The cheese can be omitted entirely for a lower fat alternative.

6 Top each half with ¼ of the goat cheese and return to the oven for a further 10–15 minutes. Garnish with snipped chives.

Zucchini and Asparagus en Papillote

An impressive dinner party accompaniment, these puffed paper parcels should be broken open at the table by each guest, so that the wonderful aroma can be fully appreciated.

Serves 4

INGREDIENTS
2 medium zucchini
1 medium leek
8 oz young asparagus, trimmed
4 tarragon sprigs
4 whole garlic cloves, unpeeled
salt and freshly ground black pepper
1 egg, beaten

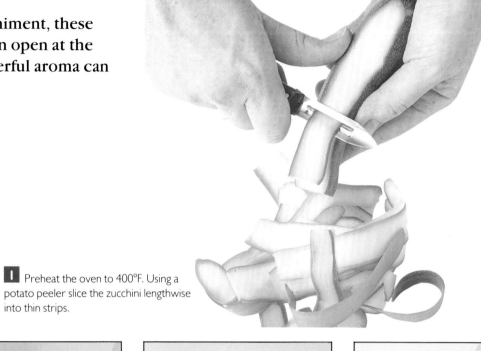

zucchini

asparagus

leek

egg

tarragon

garlic

1 Preheat the oven to 400°F. Using a potato peeler slice the zucchini lengthwise into thin strips.

2 Cut the leek into very fine julienne strips and cut the asparagus evenly into 2 in lengths.

3 Cut out 4 sheets of parchment paper 12 × 15 in in size and fold each in half. Draw a large curve to make a heart shape when unfolded. Cut along the inside of the line and open out.

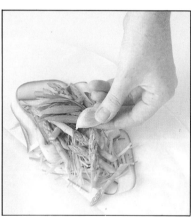

4 Divide the zucchini, asparagus and leek evenly between each paper heart, positioning the filling on one side of the fold line, and topping each with a sprig of tarragon and an unpeeled garlic clove. Season to taste.

COOK'S TIP

Experiment with other vegetables and herbs such as sugar-snap peas and mint or baby carrots and rosemary. The possibilities are endless.

5 Brush the edges lightly with the beaten egg and fold over.

6 Pleat the edges together so that each parcel is completely sealed. Lay the parcels on a cookie sheet and cook for 10 minutes. Serve immediately.

Broccoli and Chestnut Terrine

Served hot or cold, this versatile terrine is equally suitable for a dinner party as for a picnic.

Serves 4–6

INGREDIENTS
1 lb broccoli, cut into small florets
8 oz cooked chestnuts, roughly chopped
1 cup fresh wholewheat bread crumbs
4 tbsp low fat plain yogurt
2 tbsp Parmesan cheese, finely grated
salt, grated nutmeg and freshly ground black pepper
2 eggs, beaten

yogurt

bread crumbs

broccoli

chestnuts

egg

Parmesan

1 Preheat the oven to 350°F. Line a 2 lb loaf pan with a generous layer of parchment paper.

2 Blanch or steam the broccoli for 3–4 minutes until just tender. Drain well. Reserve ¼ of the smallest florets and chop the rest finely.

3 Mix together the chestnuts, bread crumbs, yogurt and Parmesan, and season to taste.

4 Fold in the chopped broccoli, reserved florets and the beaten eggs.

5 Spoon the broccoli mixture into the prepared pan.

6 Place in a roasting pan and pour in boiling water to come halfway up the sides of the loaf pan. Bake for 20–25 minutes. Remove from the oven and tip out onto a plate or tray. Serve cut into even slices.

Gado Gado

Gado Gado is a traditional Indonesian salad around which friends and family gather to eat. Fillings are chosen and wrapped in a lettuce leaf. The parcel is then dipped in a spicy peanut sauce and eaten, usually with the left hand. Salad ingredients vary according to what is in season.

Serves 4

INGREDIENTS
2 medium potatoes, peeled
salt
3 eggs
6 oz green beans, topped and tailed
1 Cos lettuce
4 tomatoes, cut into wedges
4 oz bean shoots
½ cucumber, peeled and cut into
   fingers
5 oz giant mooli, peeled and grated
6 oz tofu, cut into large dice
12 oz large cooked peeled shrimp
1 small bunch fresh cilantro

SPICY PEANUT SAUCE
½ cup smooth peanut butter
juice of ½ lemon
2 shallots or 1 small onion, finely
   chopped
1 clove garlic, crushed
1–2 small fresh red chilies, seeded and
   finely chopped
2 tbsp South-east Asian fish sauce
   (optional)
⅔ cup coconut milk, canned or fresh
1 tbsp superfine sugar

1 To make the Spicy Peanut Sauce, combine the ingredients in a food processor until smooth.

cilantro

potatoes

shrimp

Cos lettuce

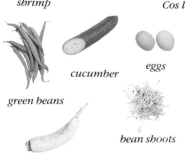

cucumber

eggs

green beans

bean shoots

mooli

2 Bring the potatoes to the boil in salted water and simmer for 20 minutes. Bring a second pan of salted water to the boil. To save using too many pans, cook the eggs and beans together: lower the eggs into the boiling water in the second pan; then, after 6 minutes, add the beans and boil for a further 6 minutes. (Hard-boiled eggs should have a total of 12 minutes.) Cool the potatoes, eggs and beans under running water.

3 Wash and spin the salad leaves and use the outer leaves to line a large platter. Pile the remainder to one side of the platter.

4 Slice the potatoes. Shell and quarter the eggs. Arrange the potatoes, eggs, beans and tomatoes in separate piles. Arrange the other salad ingredients in a similar way to cover the platter.

HANDLING CHILIES

Red chilies are considered to be sweeter and hotter than green ones. Smaller varieties of both red and green are likely to be more pungent than large varieties. You can lessen the intensity of a fresh chili by splitting it open and removing the white seed-bearing membrane. The residue given off when chilies are cut can cause serious burns to the skin. Be sure to wash your hands thoroughly after handling raw chilies and avoid touching your eyes or any sensitive skin areas.

5 Turn the Spicy Peanut Sauce into an attractive bowl and bring to the table with the salad.

Caponata

Caponata is a quintessential part of Sicilian antipasti and is a rich, spicy mixture of eggplants, tomatoes, capers and celery.

Serves 4

INGREDIENTS
4 tbsp olive oil
1 large onion, sliced
2 celery stalks, sliced
1 lb eggplant, diced
5 ripe tomatoes, chopped
1 garlic clove, crushed
3 tbsp red wine vinegar
1 tbsp sugar
2 tbsp capers
12 olives
pinch of salt
4 tbsp chopped fresh parsley,
    to garnish
warm crusty bread, to serve
olives, to serve

celery

eggplants

onion *tomatoes*

olives

capers

1 Heat half the oil in a large heavy saucepan. Add the onion and celery and cook over a gentle heat for about 3–4 minutes to soften.

2 Add the remainder of the oil with the eggplants and stir to absorb the oil. Cook until the eggplants begin to color, then add the chopped tomatoes, garlic, vinegar and sugar.

3 Cover the surface of the vegetables with a circle of waxed paper and simmer for 8–10 minutes.

4 Add the capers and olives, then season to taste with salt. Turn the caponata out into a bowl, garnish with parsley and serve at room temperature with warm crusty bread and olives.

Crispy Cabbage

This makes a wonderful accompaniment to meat or vegetable dishes – just a couple of spoonfuls will add crispy texture to a meal. It goes especially well with shrimp dishes.

Serves 2–4

INGREDIENTS
4 juniper berries
1 large Savoy cabbage
4 tbsp vegetable oil
1 clove garlic, crushed
1 tsp superfine sugar
1 tsp salt

cabbage

vegetable oil

garlic

juniper berries

1 Finely crush the juniper berries, using a pestle and mortar.

2 Finely shred the cabbage.

3 Heat the wok, then add the oil. When the oil is hot, stir-fry the garlic for 1 minute. Add the cabbage and stir-fry for 3–4 minutes until crispy. Remove and pat dry with paper towels.

4 Return the cabbage to the wok. Toss the cabbage in sugar, salt and crushed juniper berries and serve hot or cold.

Marinated Mixed Vegetables with Basil Oil

Basil oil is a must for drizzling over plain stir-fried vegetables. Once it has been made up, it will keep in the fridge for up to 2 weeks.

Serves 2–4

INGREDIENTS
1 tbsp olive oil
1 clove garlic, crushed
rind of 1 lemon, finely grated
1 × 14 oz can artichoke hearts, drained and rinsed
2 large leeks, sliced
8 oz patty pan squash, halved if large
4 oz plum tomatoes, cut into segments lengthwise
½ oz basil leaves
⅔ cup extra-virgin olive oil
salt and freshly ground black pepper

patty pan squash

artichoke hearts

leek

plum tomatoes

1 Mix together the olive oil, garlic and lemon rind in a bowl, to make a marinade.

2 Place the artichokes, leeks, patty pan squash and plum tomatoes in a large bowl, pour over the marinade and leave for 30 minutes.

3 Meanwhile, make the basil oil. Blend the basil leaves with the extra-virgin olive oil in a food processor until puréed.

4 Heat the wok, then stir-fry the marinated vegetables for 3–4 minutes, tossing well. Drizzle the basil oil over the vegetables and serve.

Red Cabbage in Port and Red Wine

A sweet and sour, spicy red cabbage dish, with the added crunch of pears and walnuts.

Serves 6

INGREDIENTS
1 tbsp walnut oil
1 onion, sliced
2 whole star anise
1 tsp ground cinnamon
pinch of ground cloves
1 lb red cabbage, finely shredded
2 tbsp dark brown sugar
3 tbsp red wine vinegar
1¼ cups red wine
⅔ cup port
2 pears, cut into ½ in cubes
½ cup raisins
salt and freshly ground black pepper
½ cup walnut halves

red cabbage
brown sugar
pears
onion
raisins
walnut halves
star anise
red wine vinegar
port
red wine

1 Heat the oil in a large pan. Add the onion and cook gently for about 5 minutes until softened.

2 Add the star anise, cinnamon, cloves and cabbage and cook for about 3 minutes more.

3 Stir in the sugar, vinegar, red wine and port. Cover the pan and simmer gently for 10 minutes, stirring occasionally.

4 Stir in the cubed pears and raisins and cook for a further 10 minutes or until the cabbage is tender. Season to taste. Mix in the walnut halves and serve.

Mooli, Beet and Carrot Stir-fry

This is a dazzling colorful dish with a crunchy texture and fragrant taste.

Serves 4

INGREDIENTS
¼ cup pine nuts
4 oz mooli, peeled
4 oz beets, peeled
4 oz carrots, peeled
1½ tsp vegetable oil
juice of 1 orange
2 tbsp fresh coriander, chopped
salt and freshly ground black pepper

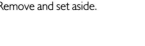

carrot

pine nuts

mooli

beet

1 Heat the wok, then add the pine nuts and toss until golden brown. remove and set on one side.

2 Cut the mooli, beets and carrots into long thin strips.

3 Heat the wok and add one-third of the oil. When the oil is hot, stir-fry the mooli, beets and carrots for 2–3 minutes. Remove and set aside.

4 Pour the orange juice into the wok and simmer for 2 minutes. Remove and keep warm.

5 Arrange the vegetables in bundles, and sprinkle over the coriander and salt and pepper.

6 Drizzle over the orange juice, sprinkle in the pine nuts, and serve.

Grilled Mixed Peppers with Feta and Green Salsa

Soft, smoky grilled peppers make a lovely combination with the slightly tart salsa.

Serves 4

INGREDIENTS

4 medium peppers in different colors
3 tbsp chopped fresh flat-leaf parsley
3 tbsp chopped fresh dill
3 tbsp chopped fresh mint
½ small red onion, finely chopped
1 tbsp capers, coarsely chopped
¼ cup Greek olives, pitted and sliced
1 fresh green chili, seeded and finely
    chopped
4 tbsp pistachios, chopped
5 tbsp extra-virgin olive oil
3 tbsp fresh lime juice
½ cup medium fat feta cheese,
    crumbled
1 oz cornichons, finely chopped

olives

feta cheese

green chili

mint

pistachios

peppers

cornichons

red onion

1 Preheat the broiler. Place the whole peppers on a tray and broil until charred and blistered.

2 Place the peppers in a plastic bag and leave to cool.

COOK'S TIP

Feta cheese is quite salty so if preferred, soak in cold water and drain well before using.

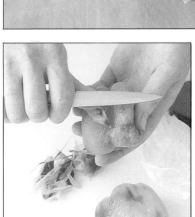

3 Peel, seed and cut the peppers into even strips.

4 Mix all the remaining ingredients together, and stir in the pepper strips.

Beet and Celeriac Gratin

Beautiful ruby-red slices of beets and celeriac make a stunning light accompaniment to any main course dish.

Serves 6

INGREDIENTS
12 oz raw beets
12 oz celeriac
4 thyme sprigs
6 juniper berries, crushed
salt and freshly ground black pepper
½ cup fresh orange juice
½ cup vegetable stock

celeriac

orange juice

juniper berries

beet

thyme

1 Preheat the oven to 375°F. Scrub, peel and slice the beets very finely. Scrub, quarter and peel the celeriac and slice very finely.

2 Fill a 10 in diameter, cast iron, ovenproof or flameproof frying pan with alternate layers of beet and celeriac slices, sprinkling with the thyme, juniper and seasoning between each layer.

3 Mix the orange juice and stock together and pour over the gratin. Place over a medium heat and bring to a boil. Boil for 2 minutes.

4 Cover with foil and place in the oven for 15–20 minutes. Remove the foil and raise the oven temperature to 400°F. Cook for a further 10 minutes until tender and bubbling.

Mixed Mushroom Ragu

These mushrooms are delicious served hot or cold and can be made up to two days in advance.

Serves 4

INGREDIENTS

1 small onion, finely chopped
1 garlic clove, crushed
1 tsp cilantro seeds, crushed
2 tbsp red wine vinegar
1 tbsp soy sauce
1 tbsp dry sherry
2 tsp tomato paste
2 tsp light brown sugar
⅔ cup vegetable stock
4 oz baby button mushrooms
4 oz cremini mushrooms, quartered
4 oz oyster mushrooms, sliced
salt and freshly ground black pepper
sprig of fresh cilantro, to garnish

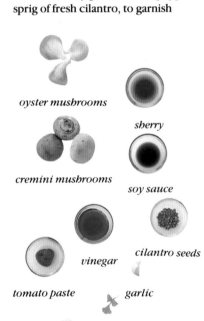

oyster mushrooms

sherry

cremini mushrooms

soy sauce

vinegar

cilantro seeds

tomato paste

garlic

cilantro

button mushrooms

onion

1 Put the first nine ingredients into a large saucepan. Bring to a boil and reduce the heat. Cover and simmer for 5 minutes.

2 Uncover the saucepan and simmer for 5 more minutes, or until the liquid has reduced by half.

3 Add the baby button and cremini mushrooms and simmer for 3 minutes. Stir in the oyster mushrooms and cook for a further 2 minutes.

4 Remove the mushrooms with a slotted spoon and transfer them to a serving dish.

5 Boil the juices for about 5 minutes, or until reduced to about 5 tbsp. Season well with salt and pepper.

6 Allow to cool for 2-3 minutes, then pour over the mushrooms. Serve hot or well chilled, garnished with fresh cilantro.

Arugula, Pear and Parmesan Salad

For a sophisticated start to an elaborate meal, try this simple salad of honey-rich pears, fresh Parmesan and aromatic leaves of arugula. Enjoy with a young Beaujolais or chilled Lambrusco wine.

Serves 4

INGREDIENTS
3 ripe pears, Williams or Packhams
2 tsp lemon juice
3 tbsp hazelnut or walnut oil
4 oz arugula leaves
3 oz Parmesan cheese, shaved
freshly ground black pepper
open-textured bread, to serve

arugula

Parmesan cheese

pears

1 Peel and core the pears and slice thickly. Moisten with lemon juice to keep the flesh white.

2 Combine the nut oil with the pears. Add the arugula leaves and toss.

3 Turn the salad out on to 4 small plates and top with shavings of Parmesan cheese. Season with freshly ground black pepper and serve.

COOK'S TIP

If you are unable to buy arugula easily, you can grow your own from early spring to late summer.

Leek and Caraway Gratin with a Carrot Crust

Tender leeks are mixed with a creamy caraway sauce and a crunchy carrot topping.

Serves 4–6

INGREDIENTS
1½ lb leeks, cut into 2 in pieces
⅔ cup fresh vegetable stock or water
3 tbsp dry white wine
1 tsp caraway seeds
pinch of salt
1¼ cups skim milk, or as required
2 tbsp butter
¼ cup plain flour

FOR THE TOPPING
2 cups fresh whole wheat
  bread crumbs
2 cups grated carrot
2 tbsp chopped fresh parsley
3 oz Jarlsberg cheese, coarsely grated
2 tbsp slivered almonds

parsley

vegetable stock

Jarlsberg

leek

bread crumbs

butter

1 Place the leeks in a large pan. Add the stock or water, wine, caraway seeds and salt. Bring to a simmer, cover and cook for 5–7 minutes until the leeks are just tender.

2 With a slotted spoon, transfer the leeks to an ovenproof dish. Reduce the remaining liquid to half then make the amount up to 1½ cups with skim milk.

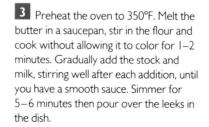

3 Preheat the oven to 350°F. Melt the butter in a saucepan, stir in the flour and cook without allowing it to color for 1–2 minutes. Gradually add the stock and milk, stirring well after each addition, until you have a smooth sauce. Simmer for 5–6 minutes then pour over the leeks in the dish.

4 Mix all the topping ingredients together in a bowl and sprinkle over the leeks. Bake for 20–25 minutes until golden.

Apple Coleslaw

The term coleslaw stems from the Dutch *koolsla*, meaning 'cool cabbage'. There are many variations of this salad; this recipe combines the sweet flavors of apple and carrot with celery salt. Coleslaw is traditionally served with cold ham.

Serves 4

INGREDIENTS
1 lb white cabbage
1 medium onion
2 apples, peeled and cored
6 oz carrots, peeled
⅔ cup mayonnaise
1 tsp celery salt
freshly ground black pepper

carrots

onion

apple

white cabbage

1 Discard the outside leaves of the cabbage if they are dirty, cut the cabbage into 2 in wedges, then remove the stem section.

2 Feed the cabbage and the onion through a food processor fitted with a slicing blade. Change to a grating blade and grate the apples and carrots. Alternatively use a hand grater and vegetable slicer.

3 Combine the salad ingredients in a large bowl. Fold in the mayonnaise and season with celery salt and freshly ground black pepper.

COOK'S TIP

This recipe can be adapted easily to suit different tastes. You could add ½ cup chopped walnuts or raisins for added texture. For a richer coleslaw, add ½ cup grated Cheddar cheese. You may find you will need smaller portions, as the cheese makes a more filling dish.

Sweet Turnip Salad with Horseradish and Caraway

The robust-flavored turnip partners well with the taste of horseradish and caraway seeds. This salad is delicous with cold roast beef and smoked trout.

Serves 4

INGREDIENTS
12 oz medium turnips
2 scallions, white part only, chopped
1 tbsp superfine sugar
salt
2 tbsp horseradish cream
2 tsp caraway seeds

turnips

scallions

COOK'S TIP
If turnips are not available, mooli can be used as a substitute.

1 Peel, slice and shred the turnips – or grate them if you wish.

2 Add the scallions, sugar and salt, then rub together with your hands to soften the turnip.

3 Fold in the horseradish cream and caraway seeds.

Strawberry Conchiglie Salad with Kirsch and Raspberry Sauce

A divinely decadent dessert laced with liqueur and luscious raspberry sauce.

Serves 4

INGREDIENTS
6 oz pasta shells (conchiglie)
salt
½ lb fresh or frozen raspberries, thawed if frozen
1–2 tbsp superfine sugar
lemon juice
1 lb small fresh strawberries
flaked almonds
3 tbsp kirsch

pasta shells

raspberries

strawberries

almonds

1 Cook the pasta in plenty of boiling salted water according to the manufacturer's instructions. Drain well and cool.

2 Purée the raspberries in a food processor and pass through a strainer to remove the seeds.

3 Put the purée in a small saucepan with the sugar and simmer for 5–6 minutes, stirring occasionally. Add lemon juice to taste. Set aside to cool.

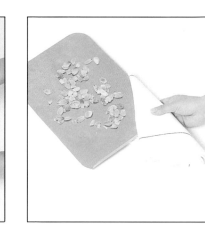

4 Hull the strawberries and halve if necessary. Toss with the pasta and transfer to a serving bowl.

5 Spread the almonds on a baking sheet and toast under the broiler until golden. Cool.

6 Stir the kirsch into the raspberry sauce and pour over the salad. Scatter with the toasted almonds and serve.

Apricot Delight

A fluffy mousse base with a layer of fruit jelly on top makes this dessert doubly delicious.

Serves 8

INGREDIENTS
2 × 14 oz cans apricots in natural juice
4 tbsp fructose
1 tbsp lemon juice
5 tsp powdered gelatin
15 oz low fat ready made custard
⅔ cup strained yogurt
yogurt piping cream to decorate
1 apricot, sliced and sprig of fresh apple mint, to decorate

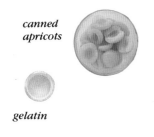

canned apricots

gelatin

custard

strained yogurt

1 Line the base of a 5 cup heart-shaped cake pan with non-stick baking paper.

2 Drain the apricots, reserving the juice. Put the drained apricots in a food processor or blender fitted with a metal blade together with the fructose and 4 tbsp of the apricot juice. Blend to a smooth purée.

3 Measure 2 tbsp of the apricot juice into a small bowl. Add the lemon juice, then sprinkle over 2 tsp of the gelatin. Leave for about 5 minutes, until 'spongy'.

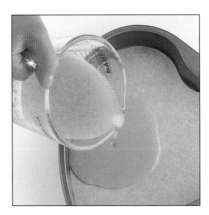

4 Stir the gelatin into half of the purée and pour into the prepared pan. Chill in a refrigerator for 1½ hours, or until firm.

COOK'S TIP

Don't use a loose-bottomed cake pan for this recipe as the mixture may seep through before it sets.

5 Sprinkle the remaining 1 tbsp of gelatin over 4 tbsp of the apricot juice. Soak and dissolve as before. Mix the remaining apricot purée with the custard, yogurt and gelatine. Pour onto the layer of set fruit purée and chill in the refrigerator for 3 hours.

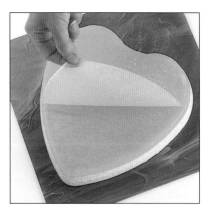

6 Dip the cake pan into hot water for a few seconds and unmold the delice onto a serving plate. Decorate with yogurt piping cream, the sliced apricot and sprigs of fresh apple mint.

Raspberry Salad with Mango Custard Sauce

This remarkable salad unites the sharp quality of fresh raspberries with a special custard made from rich fragrant mangoes.

Serves 4

INGREDIENTS
1 large mango
3 egg yolks
2 tbsp superfine sugar
2 tsp cornflour
scant 1 cup skimmed milk
8 sprigs fresh mint

RASPBERRY SAUCE
1 lb 2 oz raspberries
3 tbsp superfine sugar

eggs

mint

mango

raspberries

COOK'S TIP

Mangoes are ripe when they yield to gentle pressure in the hand. Some varieties show a red-gold or yellow flush when they are ready to eat.

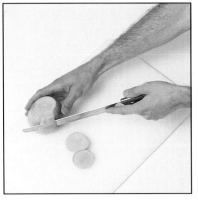

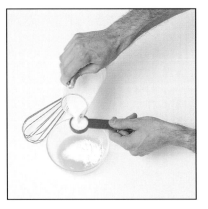

1 To prepare the mango, remove the top and bottom with a serrated knife. Cut away the outer skin, then remove the flesh by cutting either side of the flat central stone. Save one half of the fruit for decoration and roughly chop the remainder.

2 For the custard, combine the egg yolks, sugar, cornflour and 2 tbsp of the milk smoothly in a bowl.

3 Rinse a small saucepan out with cold water to prevent the milk from catching. Bring the rest of the milk to the boil in the pan, pour it over the ingredients in the bowl and stir evenly.

4 Sieve the mixture back into the saucepan, stir to a simmer and allow the mixture to thicken.

5 Pour the custard into a food processor, add the chopped mango and blend until smooth. Allow to cool.

6 To make the raspberry sauce, place 12 oz of the raspberries in a stain-resistant saucepan. Add the sugar, soften over a gentle heat and simmer for 5 minutes. Rub the fruit through a fine nylon sieve to remove the seeds. Allow to cool.

7 Spoon the raspberry sauce and mango custard into 2 pools on 4 plates. Slice the reserved mango and fan out or arrange in a pattern over the raspberry sauce. Scatter fresh raspberries over the mango custard. Decorate with 2 sprigs of mint and serve.

Iced Pineapple Crush with Strawberries and Lychees

The sweet tropical flavors of pineapple and lychees combine well with richly scented strawberries to make this a most refreshing salad.

Serves 4

INGREDIENTS
2 small pineapples
1 lb strawberries
14 oz can lychees
3 tbsp Kirsch or white rum
2 tbsp confectioners' sugar

pineapple

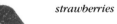

strawberries

1 Remove the crown from both pineapples by twisting sharply. Reserve the leaves for decoration.

2 Cut the fruit in half diagonally with a large serrated knife.

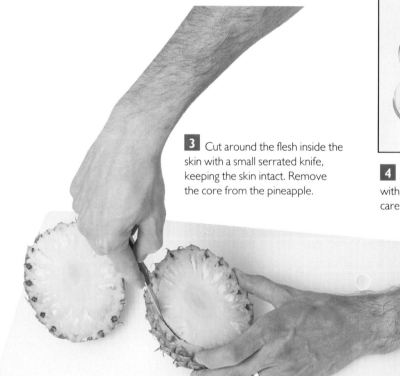

3 Cut around the flesh inside the skin with a small serrated knife, keeping the skin intact. Remove the core from the pineapple.

4 Chop the pineapple and combine with the strawberries and lychees, taking care not to damage the fruit.

COOK'S TIP
A ripe pineapple will resist pressure when squeezed and will have a sweet, fragrant smell. In winter freezing conditions can cause the flesh to blacken.

5 Combine the Kirsch with the confectioners' sugar, pour over the fruit and freeze for 45 minutes.

6 Turn the fruit out into the pineapple skins and decorate with pineapple leaves.

Watermelon Sorbet

A slice of this refreshing sorbet is the perfect way to cool down on a hot sunny day.

Serves 4–6

INGREDIENTS
½ small watermelon, weighing about
   2¼ lb
½ cup superfine sugar
4 tbsp cranberry juice or water
2 tbsp lemon juice
sprigs of fresh mint, to decorate

cranberry juice

sugar

watermelon   lemon juice

1 Cut the watermelon into 4–6 equal-sized wedges (depending on the number of servings you require). Scoop out the pink flesh, discarding the seeds but reserving the shell.

2 Line a freezer-proof bowl, about the same size as the melon, with plastic wrap. Arrange the melon skins in the bowl to re-form the shell, fitting them together snugly so that there are no gaps. Put in the freezer.

3 Put the sugar and cranberry juice or water in a saucepan and stir over a low heat until the sugar dissolves. Bring to a boil and simmer for 5 minutes. Leave the sugar syrup to cool.

4 Put the melon flesh and lemon juice in a blender and process to a smooth purée. Stir in the sugar syrup and pour into a freezer-proof container. Freeze for 3–3½ hours, or until slushy.

5 Tip the sorbet into a chilled bowl and whisk to break up the ice crystals. Return to the freezer for another 30 minutes, whisk again, then tip into the melon shell and freeze until solid.

6 Remove from the freezer and leave to defrost at room temperature for 15 minutes. Take the melon out of the bowl and cut into wedges with a warmed sharp knife. Serve with sprigs of fresh mint.

COOK'S TIP

If preferred, this pretty pink sorbet can be served scooped into balls. Do this before the mixture is completely frozen and re-freeze the balls on a baking sheet, ready to serve.

Mango and Coconut Stir-fry

Choose a ripe mango for this recipe. If you buy one
that is a little under-ripe, leave it in a warm place for a
day or two before using.

Serves 4

INGREDIENTS
¼ coconut
1 large, ripe mango
juice of 2 limes
rind of 2 limes, finely grated
1 tbsp sunflower oil
1 tbsp butter
1½ tbsp honey
sour cream or yogurt, to serve

coconut

mango

honey

lime

COOK'S TIP

Because of the delicate taste of
desserts, always make sure your wok
has been scrupulously cleaned so
there is no transference of flavors – a
garlicky mango isn't quite the effect
you want to achieve!

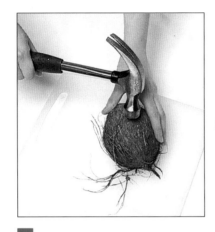

1 Prepare the coconut shreds by
draining the milk from the coconut and
shredding the flesh with a peeler.

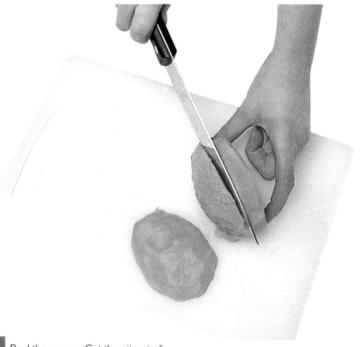

2 Peel the mango. Cut the pit out of
the middle of the fruit. Cut each half of
the mango into slices.

3 Place the mango slices in a bowl and
pour over the lime juice and rind, to
marinate them.

4 Meanwhile, heat the wok, then add
2 tsp of the oil. When the oil is hot, add
the butter. When the butter has melted,
stir in the coconut shreds and stir-fry for
1–2 minutes until the coconut is golden
brown. Remove and drain on paper
towels. Wipe out the wok. Strain the
mango slices, reserving the juice.

5 Heat the wok and add the remaining
oil. When the oil is hot, add the mango
and stir-fry for 1–2 minutes, then add the
juice and allow to bubble and reduce for
1 minute. Then stir in the honey, sprinkle
on the coconut and serve with sour
cream or yogurt.

Feather-light Peach Pudding

On chilly days, try this hot fruit pudding with its tantalizing sponge topping.

Serves 4

INGREDIENTS

14 oz can peach slices in
 natural juice
4 tbsp low fat spread
¼ cup light brown sugar
1 egg, beaten
½ cup plain whole wheat
 flour
½ cup flour
1 tsp baking powder
½ tsp ground cinnamon
4 tbsp skim milk
½ tsp vanilla extract
2 tsp confectioner's sugar, for
 dusting
low fat ready-made custard,
 to serve

peach slices

flour

*confectioner's
sugar*

egg

brown sugar

*low fat
custard*

I Preheat the oven to 350°F. Drain the peaches and put into a 4 cup pie dish with 2 tbsp of the juice.

2 Put all the remaining ingredients, except the confectioner's sugar into a mixing bowl. Beat for 3–4 minutes, until thoroughly combined.

Cook's Tip

For a simple sauce, blend 1 tsp arrowroot with 1 tbsp peach juice in a small saucepan. Stir in the remaining peach juice from the can and bring to a boil. Simmer for 1 minute until thickened and clear.

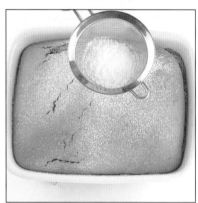

3 Spoon the sponge mixture over the peaches and level the top evenly. Cook in the oven for 35-40 minutes, or until springy to the touch.

4 Lightly dust the top with confectioner's sugar and serve hot with the low fat custard.

Plum, Rum and Raisin Brulée

Crack through the crunchy caramel to find the juicy plums and smooth creamy center of this dessert.

Serves 4

INGREDIENTS
3 tbsp raisins
1 tbsp dark rum
12 oz medium plums (about 6)
juice of 1 orange
1 tbsp honey
2 cups low fat cream cheese
½ cup sugar

raisins

rum

orange

plums

honey

1 Put the raisins into a small bowl and sprinkle over the rum. Leave to soak for 5 minutes.

2 Quarter the plums and remove their pits. Put into a large, heavy-based saucepan together with the orange juice and honey. Simmer gently for 5 minutes or until soft. Stir in the soaked raisins. Reserve 1 tbsp of the juice, then divide the rest between four ⅔ cup ramekin dishes.

3 Blend the low fat cream cheese with the reserved 1 tbsp of plum juice. Spoon over the plums and chill in the refrigerator for 1 hour.

4 Put the sugar into a large, heavy-based saucepan with 3 tbsp cold water. Heat gently, stirring, until the sugar has dissolved. Boil for 15 minutes or until it turns golden brown. Cool for 2 minutes, then carefully pour over the ramekins. Cool and serve.

Blushing Pears

Pears poached in rosé wine and sweet spices absorb all the subtle flavors and turn a soft pink color.

Serves 6

INGREDIENTS
6 firm pears
1¼ cups rosé wine
⅔ cup cranberry or clear apple
   juice
strip of thinly pared orange rind
1 cinnamon stick
4 whole cloves
1 bay leaf
5 tbsp superfine sugar
small bay leaves, to decorate

wine

pears

cranberry juice

cinnamon

sugar

orange

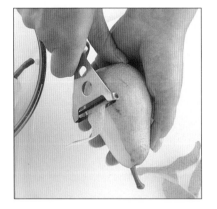

1 Thinly peel the pears with a sharp knife or vegetable peeler, leaving the stems attached.

2 Pour the wine and cranberry or apple juice into a large heavy-based saucepan. Add the orange rind, cinnamon stick, cloves, bay leaf and sugar.

3 Heat gently, stirring all the time until the sugar has dissolved. Add the pears and stand them upright in the pan. Pour in enough cold water to barely cover them. Cover and cook very gently for 20–30 minutes, or until just tender, turning and basting occasionally.

4 Using a slotted spoon, gently lift the pears out of the syrup and transfer to a serving dish.

5 Bring the syrup to a boil and boil rapidly for 10–15 minutes, or until it has reduced by half.

COOK'S TIP

Check the pears by piercing with a skewer or sharp knife towards the end of the poaching time because some may cook more quickly than others.

6 Strain the syrup and pour over the pears. Serve hot or well-chilled, decorated with bay leaves.

Carrot and Zucchini Cake

If you can't resist the lure of a slice of iced cake, you'll love this moist, spiced sponge cake with its delicious creamy topping.

Serves 10

INGREDIENTS
1 medium carrot
1 medium zucchini
3 eggs, separated
scant ½ cup light brown
   sugar
2 tbsp ground almonds
finely grated rind of 1 orange
1 cup self-rising whole wheat flour
1 tsp ground cinnamon
fondant carrots and zucchini, to
   decorate

FOR THE TOPPING
¾ cup low fat cream cheese
1 tsp honey

fondant decorations

egg

cinnamon

zucchini

brown sugar

carrot

orange

honey

1 Preheat the oven to 350°F. Line a 7 in square pan with non-stick baking paper. Coarsely grate the carrot and zucchini.

2 Put the egg yolks, sugar, ground almonds and orange rind into a bowl and whisk until very thick and light.

3 Sift together the flour and cinnamon and fold into the mixture together with the grated vegetables. Add any bran left over from the flour in the sieve.

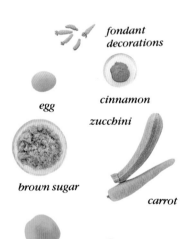

4 Whisk the egg whites until stiff and carefully fold them in, a half at a time. Spoon into the prepared pan. Bake in the oven for 1 hour and cover the top with foil after 40 minutes.

5 Leave to cool in the tin for 5 minutes, then turn out onto a wire rack and carefully remove the lining paper.

6 For the topping, beat together the cheese and honey and spread over the cake. Decorate with fondant carrots and zucchini.

Cheese and Chive Scones

Feta cheese makes an excellent substitute for butter in these tangy savory scones.

Makes 9

INGREDIENTS
1 cup self-rising flour
1 cup self-rising whole wheat flour
½ tsp salt
3 oz feta cheese
1 tbsp snipped fresh chives
⅔ cup skim milk, plus extra for
  glazing
¼ tsp cayenne pepper

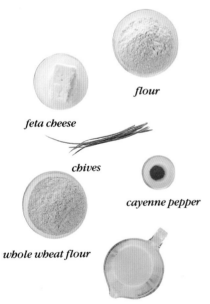

flour

feta cheese

chives

cayenne pepper

whole wheat flour

milk

1 Preheat the oven to 400°F. Sift the flours and salt into a mixing bowl, adding any bran left over from the flour in the sieve.

2 Crumble the feta cheese and rub into the dry ingredients. Stir in the chives, then add the milk and mix to a soft dough.

3 Turn out onto a floured surface and lightly knead until smooth. Roll out to ¾ in thick and stamp out nine scones with a 2½ in cookie cutter.

4 Transfer the scones to a non-stick baking sheet. Brush with skim milk, then sprinkle over the cayenne pepper. Bake in the oven for 15 minutes, or until golden brown. Serve warm or cold.

Sage Soda Bread

This wonderful loaf, quite unlike bread made with yeast, has a velvety texture and a powerful sage aroma.

Makes 1 loaf

INGREDIENTS
2 cups whole wheat flour
1 cup flour
½ tsp salt
1 tsp baking soda
2 tbsp shredded fresh sage or 2 tsp
   dried sage, crumbled
1¼–1¾ cups buttermilk

white flour

whole wheat flour

sage

buttermilk

1 Preheat the oven to 425°F. Sift the dry ingredients into a bowl.

2 Stir in the sage and add enough buttermilk to make a soft dough.

COOK'S TIP

As an alternative to the sage, try using finely chopped rosemary or thyme.

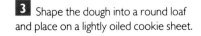

3 Shape the dough into a round loaf and place on a lightly oiled cookie sheet.

4 Cut a deep cross in the top. Bake in the oven for 40 minutes until the loaf is well risen and sounds hollow when tapped on the bottom. Leave to cool on a wire rack.

Chocolate and Orange Angel Cake

This light-as-air cake with its fluffy icing is virtually fat free, yet tastes heavenly.

Serves 10

INGREDIENTS
¼ cup flour
2 tbsp reduced fat cocoa powder
2 tbsp cornstarch
pinch of salt
5 egg whites
½ tsp cream of tartar
scant ½ cup superfine sugar
blanched and shredded rind of 1
    orange, to decorate

ICING
1 cup superfine sugar
1 egg white

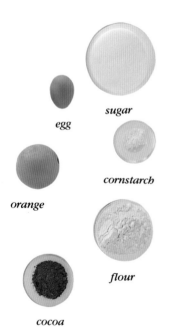

1 Preheat the oven to 350°F. Sift the flour, cocoa powder, cornstarch and salt together three times. Beat the egg whites in a large bowl until foamy. Add the cream of tartar, then whisk until soft peaks form.

2 Add the superfine sugar to the egg whites a spoonful at a time, whisking after each addition. Sift a third of the flour and cocoa mixture over the meringue and gently fold in. Repeat, sifting and folding in the flour and cocoa mixture two more times.

3 Spoon the mixture into a non-stick 8 in ring mold and level the top. Bake in the oven for 35 minutes or until springy when lightly pressed. Turn upsidedown onto a wire rack and leave to cool in the tin. Carefully ease out of the pan.

4 For the icing, put the sugar in a pan with 5 tbsp cold water. Stir over a low heat until dissolved. Boil until the syrup reaches a temperature of 240°F on a sugar thermometer, or when a drop of the syrup makes a soft ball when dropped into a cup of cold water. Remove from the heat.

5 Whisk the egg white until stiff. Add the syrup in a thin stream, whisking all the time. Continue to whisk until the mixture is very thick and fluffy.

COOK'S TIP

Make sure you do not over-beat the egg whites. They should not be stiff but should form soft peaks, so that the air bubbles can expand further during cooking and help the cake to rise.

6 Spread the icing over the top and sides of the cooled cake. Sprinkle the orange rind over the top of the cake and serve.

Zucchini and Walnut Loaf

Cardamom seeds impart their distinctive aroma to this loaf. Serve spread with ricotta and honey for a delicious snack.

Makes 1 loaf

INGREDIENTS
3 eggs
⅓ cup light brown sugar, firmly packed
½ cup sunflower oil
2 cups whole wheat flour
1 tsp baking powder
1 tsp baking soda
1 tsp ground cinnamon
¾ tsp ground allspice
½ tbsp green cardamoms, seeds removed and crushed
5 oz zucchini, coarsely grated
½ cup walnuts, chopped
¼ cup sunflower seeds

zucchini

walnuts

egg

sunflower oil

brown sugar

whole wheat flour

sunflower seeds

cardamom pods

1 Preheat the oven to 350°F. Line the base and sides of a 2 lb loaf pan with parchment paper.

2 Beat the eggs and sugar together and gradually add the oil.

3 Sift the flour into a bowl together with the baking powder, baking soda, cinnamon and allspice.

4 Mix into the egg mixture with the rest of the ingredients, reserving 1 tbsp of the sunflower seeds for the top.

5 Spoon into the loaf tin, level off the top, and sprinkle with the reserved sunflower seeds.

6 Bake for 1 hour or until a skewer inserted in the center comes out clean. Leave to cool slightly before turning out onto a wire rack to cool completely.

Saffron Focaccia

A dazzling yellow bread that is light in texture and distinctive in flavor.

Makes 1 loaf

INGREDIENTS
pinch of saffron threads
⅔ cup boiling water
2 cups flour
½ tsp salt
1 tsp easy-blend dry yeast
1 tbsp olive oil

FOR THE TOPPING
2 garlic cloves, sliced
1 red onion, cut into thin wedges
rosemary sprigs
12 black olives, pitted and coarsely
   chopped
1 tbsp olive oil

flour

garlic

rosemary

red onion

olives

saffron

yeast

1 Place the saffron in a heatproof cup and pour on the boiling water. Leave to stand and infuse until lukewarm.

2 Place the flour, salt, yeast and olive oil in a food processor. Turn on and gradually add the saffron and its liquid. Process until the dough forms into a ball.

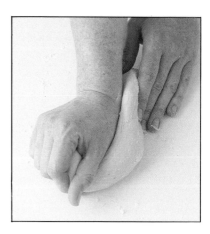

3 Turn onto a floured board and knead for 10–15 minutes. Place in a bowl, cover and leave to rise for 30–40 minutes until doubled in size.

4 Punch down the risen dough on a lightly floured surface and roll out into an oval shape, ½ in thick. Place on a lightly greased cookie sheet and leave to rise for 20–30 minutes.

5 Preheat the oven to 400°F. Press small indentations all over the surface of the focaccia with your fingers.

6 Cover with the topping ingredients, brush lightly with olive oil, and bake for 25 minutes or until the loaf sounds hollow when tapped on the bottom. Leave to cool on a wire rack.

INDEX